Everyday God

Paula Gooder is a freelance writer and lecturer in biblical studies. She is Canon Theologian of Birmingham Cathedral, a Reader in the Church of England, and a member of General Synod.

Her numerous books include *The Meaning is in the Waiting: The Spirit of Advent* (Canterbury Press), *Lentwise: Spiritual Essentials for Real Life* (Church House Publishing), and *Exploring New Testament Greek: A Way In* (SCM Press).

She lives in Birmingham.

Everyday God

The Spirit of the Ordinary

Paula Gooder

Fortress Press
Minneapolis

EVERYDAY GOD
The Spirit of the Ordinary

Fortress Press Edition © 2015

The R. S. Thomas poem 'The Bright Field' is from *Collected Poems:
1945–1990*, 2000, and is reproduced by permission of Orion Books.

Scripture quotations are from the New Revised Standard Version of
the Bible, copyright 1989 by the Division of Christian Education of
the National Council of the Churches of Christ in the USA. Used by
permission. All rights reserved.

Cover design: Laurie Ingram
Cover image: *Time, Worn Steps* © Will Bergkamp
Author photo: Abha Thakor

Library of Congress Cataloging-in-Publication Data is available
Print ISBN: 978-1-4514-9805-9
eBook ISBN: 978-1-4514-9807-3

The paper used in this publication meets the minimum requirements
of American National Standard for Information Sciences —
Permanence of Paper for Printed Library Materials, ANSI
Z329.48-1984.

Manufactured in the U.S.

For Rachel Christophers,
whose extraordinary wisdom
has helped me to love the ordinary

For Rachel Christophers,
whose extraordinary wisdom
has helped me to love the ordinary

CONTENTS

HOW TO READ
THIS BOOK

The problem with writing a book about ordinariness is that it risks being seen as thoroughly boring. The theme doesn't suggest excitement in any shape or form. Ordinariness is not exhilarating; it does not imply stimulation or interest. Surely ordinariness is something to be shunned in favour of things that are special, newer, bigger and better? The difficulty with this, however, is that while occasionally we can indulge in special, exciting, bigger and better events, a large part of our life *is* ordinary. It doesn't really matter how glamorous (or not) your life is, you still need to do ordinary things like travelling to work, brushing your teeth or doing the weekly shop. We all have long periods of ordinariness and in these periods is a richness, a depth of potential experience which we need to encounter. This book seeks to take the time to savour ordinariness and to discern a little more what a spirituality of ordinariness might look like. It seeks to encounter again not only the importance of ordinariness but the inspiration that we can gain from a deeper and more sustained reflection on the everyday.

This book falls into what is slowly becoming a series. The series began with a book on Advent, *The Meaning is in the Waiting: The Spirit of Advent*, which I was asked to write. I enjoyed it so much that I begged my publisher to let me write another based around my favourite season of Easter, *This Risen Existence: The Spirit of Easter*. Then, having done two, the series took on a life of its own in my head and almost before I was conscious of it, I asked whether I could tack on something on the longest season of the church's year, known as Ordinary Time.[1]

Books such as these are not designed to tell you everything you need to know about Advent, Easter or Ordinary Time – there are plenty of other books that do that much better than this one could. Nor are they designed to go through expounding the lectionary readings for people preparing to preach; again Christian bookshops are full of such volumes. Instead, in this book, as much as in the Advent and Easter books, I am trying to capture an essence, to communicate a feeling about a season which may help us to encounter that season more intentionally and with a clearer insight into what we might learn about God and ourselves during that season.

Of course Ordinary Time is probably the soggiest season of all. Very few if any people enter Ordinary Time with any intention other than allowing it to slide by until the Kingdom season and Advent hove into view once more. Few people are even conscious that they are in Ordinary Time when they are. Nevertheless it is a good time of the year to stop and reflect about the importance of ordinariness. I remain passionately convinced that we need to look again at a spirituality of ordinariness because without a proper understanding of the importance of ordinariness, our lives become an impoverished waiting room, as we loiter between one big event and another.

It doesn't matter at all whether you are reading this book in Ordinary Time or not; it doesn't even matter if you have never even heard of Ordinary Time. What is important is the celebration of the ordinary in all its

1 For a fuller description of what Ordinary Time is see pages 6–7.

forms: in the lives of ordinary people; in a God who defies our best attempts to put him in a gilded palace; in a kingdom that is best likened to seeds, yeast and fishing nets, and in everyday decisions which, lived out with God, have extraordinary consequences. I have no desire whatsoever to strip out of our lives a sense of awe and wonder, merely to remind us all that majesty can be found in the everyday just as much as in the splendour of regal palaces, and that extraordinariness can just as easily be observed in ordinary as in special things.

I have chosen in this book to look at the theme of ordinariness through the lens of thirty-three biblical passages which all, in some way or another, touch on the theme of ordinariness. There is no great mystical significance to the number thirty-three, it is simply the number of weeks in Ordinary Time in most years. I do not for a moment expect that anyone will read one reflection a week throughout the periods of Ordinary Time but they are here to be dipped in and out of as suits your own pattern.

As in the other two books in this series (Advent and Easter), for the most part I deal with texts in their final form. Although, as an avid student of the Bible myself, I am fascinated by questions of how the biblical books reached their final form, I am all too aware that this interest is, to put it mildly, not shared by everyone. So, as far as possible, I have left overtly critical questions aside, only bringing them in as and when they are particularly important for understanding a specific text. Each chapter of the book is split into a number of sections. In most chapters there are six sections but since six does not go into thirty-three the final chapter has only three. Each section is headed by the specific passage that I will be reflecting on but also with the suggestion for further reading if, like me, you like to read a passage in context. Sometimes there is no easy wider context to suggest, and in those cases I haven't suggested any, but for the most part there are longer bits of reading to do for those who would like to.

Also, as in the other volumes in this series, I have chosen an R. S. Thomas poem as an additional lens through which to view the essence of ordinariness. The poem 'The Bright Field' (which you will find at the start of the Introduction below) introduces something which is for me a vital strand to the whole question of ordinariness. This is the need for us to be people who can turn aside in order to encounter God. Indeed, it is so important that Chapter 1 focuses around this whole question, before we turn outwards to questions of the unsung heroes of the Bible, the ordinariness of God and his kingdom, living extra-ordinary ordinary lives and, finally, catching glimpses of God's glory in our everyday lives.

Introduction

REFLECTIONS ON THE IMPORTANCE OF BEING ORDINARY

The Bright Field

I have seen the sun break through
to illuminate a small field
for a while, and gone my way
and forgotten it. But that was the pearl
of great price, the one field that had
treasure in it. I realize now
that I must give all that I have
to possess it. Life is not hurrying
on to a receding future, nor hankering after
an imagined past. It is the turning
aside like Moses to the miracle
of the lit bush, to a brightness
that seemed as transitory as your youth
once, but is the eternity that awaits you.

R. S. Thomas

Where has Ordinary gone?

Ordinary is out of fashion; so much so, in fact, that calling something 'ordinary' suggests that it is somehow substandard, disappointing and certainly lacklustre. We might say that the food in a certain restaurant is 'ordinary'; that the clothes we have on are just something 'ordinary'; or of a football team that their performance was 'ordinary'. What we mean by this is that the food in the restaurant doesn't live up to our expectations, that our outfit is nothing special or that the football team could have done better. Describing something as ordinary isn't quite an insult but it certainly isn't a compliment. This dissatisfaction with ordinariness is, perhaps, summed up in the inspection of schools, where a school inspector can deem the institution to be excellent, good, satisfactory or unsatisfactory. Anyone in education will tell you that it is not satisfactory to be deemed satisfactory. In other words, ordinary is simply not good enough.

On one level I relate to this entirely. There is something vitally important about aiming for excellence in all that we do. The only adequate response to the God of infinite care and generosity is, in our finite way, to meet his extravagance with the very best of who we are and what we have. The pursuit of our own excellence (not in comparison with others but simply the best we can do) is surely the human vocation in response to God's great goodness.

Nevertheless, you can't help wondering whether our desire for excellence has got out of control and has, in some ways, become a monster that consumes us rather than a natural response to God's goodness. In marketing, things are constantly branded as 'all new', 'best ever' or '20% bigger', as though we simply cannot buy something unless it is demonstrably better, bigger and more attractive than before. Our expectations these days are constantly angled towards the expectation that whatever we do today will be more exciting and more satisfying than yesterday. It sometimes causes me to pause in the supermarket, with my hand hovering over the hand wash (or other similar substance) and to wonder whether I really need it to be better and more exciting than my previous one. Since my old hand wash washed my hands, made them smell nice, moisturized AND killed all the bacteria, is there anything more left for this new improved, all new recipe, 50% bigger hand wash to achieve?

The time when this really rankles with me is in coffee shops. I can't drink a lot of coffee so would prefer to have a 'regular' or even, shocking as though this might sound, a 'small' cup of coffee. This, however, is not vouchsafed in most large chain coffee shops where your choice begins with 'tall' and moves upwards from there. Starbucks, I read, has now even introduced a fourth size of coffee in the USA, called the Trente, which contains 31 ounces or 916 ml of liquid, in other words 16 ml bigger than the average human stomach. Where, I wonder, can we go from here? What happens when 'bigger and better' becomes either unfeasible or undesirable?

Ordinary, it seems, is no longer. We now move ever onwards from big to bigger, from good to better, from exciting to more exciting. Ordinary is dull, unsatisfactory and to be avoided at all costs.

Why Ordinariness is essential

It is easy to parody this kind of attitude but it has a grip on us that it makes it hard for us to escape, even in church. The major Christian festivals such as Christmas and Easter have always, and rightly, been occasions of much focus and celebration within the church. The problem is not our celebration of major festivals, nor even particular times leading up to them such as Advent and Lent. The problem is what we do in between. What do we do on 'ordinary' days, whether they be Sundays or any other day of the week? What do we do on days that aren't special?

It is tempting either to focus entirely on the special days so that we wish the days away until those special days come round again or to attempt to make every day special so that there are no ordinary days left. Neither helps us to get in touch with ordinariness. In my view ordinariness is essential to our well-being as people and a vital part of our life in Christ. We need the ordinary in order to help us fully to encounter the extraordinary. It would be impossible to appreciate the light in a painting without any less bright shades. If it really were Christmas every day, as the song written by the glam-rock band Wizzard wishes with such fervour, then Christmas itself would lose its appeal let alone its meaning. Almost by definition, if things are special all the time they become the new ordinary and we then need to think up ever grander ways of being special. Ordinariness is the canvas against which we can appreciate the special and it helps us to appreciate much more deeply the meaning of days, events or moments that are extraordinary.

Even more than this, however, ordinariness is the very essence of existence. We live the vast majority of our time in ordinariness. It is hard to make brushing your teeth, washing up or going to work every day glamorous, largely because they are not. They are the stuff of everyday living. They aren't exciting but they are necessary. Our daily existence is one of ordinariness and we doom ourselves to a life of dissatisfaction and disappointment if we cannot find some way of living contentedly with the everyday.

Seeing where the treasure lies

As with so many things, the quality of the lives we live is shaped not so much by *what* we do but by *how* we do it. It is so easy to trudge through life, simply missing the gems and wonder of everyday existence, not because they are absent but because we don't notice them. I remember an occasion when my daughters were small, when one of them squealed in ecstasy, saying, 'Look, Mummy, look.' I looked and what I saw was a somewhat grubby patch of grass – with rather more mud than makes a parent, who has to do the washing, happy – which was dotted with a few, to my eye, miserable looking daisies. She hopped out of the pushchair and rushed over to them, and crouched down as low as she could get. 'Look,' she said, 'they've got pink edges right on the end, and the petals are like a fan and the yellow bit is all furry.'

She was, of course, right, as anyone who has examined a daisy up close will tell you. What she was even more right about was that the somewhat ordinary muddy patch of grass held a treasure which I had completely overlooked. This is expressed much better than I could ever do by Saunders Lewis in his poem 'A Daisy in April'

Yesterday I saw a daisy
Like a shining mirror of the dawn.
The day before I walked over it without thought.
Yesterday I saw.

This is also one of the themes that R. S. Thomas was exploring in his poem, 'The Bright Field' (on page 1). The poem recalls Thomas's experience of seeing sunlight breaking through onto a field but only subsequently realizing that the field contained the treasure for which he yearned, so constrained was he by hurrying onwards to a 'receding future' or 'hankering after an imagined past'. We might add to this list looking upwards to heaven (or our modern equivalent) and waiting for a grand divine display of magnificence. What R. S. Thomas is reflecting on is that we all too easily hurry past the pearls of great price that lie along our way because we simply don't recognize them for what they are. Our vision remains so dazzled by an imagined future glory or a rose-tinted memory of the past that we fail to notice what lies before our very eyes.

One of the great dangers of becoming too sucked into a culture that glories in everything new, bigger and better is that it can – indeed it seeks to – take the shine away from what we already have. If 'special' is what we aim for, then by extension 'ordinary' is disappointing. The problem with this is that sometimes – often in fact – the special is embedded deep within the ordinary but it takes a well-trained eye to notice it.

Ordinary Time

For churches that use the lectionary, the problem of what we do with ordinariness becomes focused in what is now often called Ordinary Time. The problem is not unique, however, to churches which use the lectionary. All churches face the challenge of what to do, week after week, month after month in ordinary services when nothing particularly 'special' happens. Even if you happen to attend a church which manages to feel special every week of the year, the question remains of what you do in between, during the week, on a Monday morning, perhaps, in the middle of winter or Tuesday afternoon during a damp rainy summer. The liturgical season of Ordinary Time simply shines a spotlight on an experience that we all have at some point in our Christian life, when following Jesus becomes a part of the everyday routine of our daily lives.

The term Ordinary Time is used to refer to a stretch of Sundays between the major seasons. There are two sections of Ordinary Time in the Church's calendar: one, a shorter one, falls between Epiphany and the start of Lent and another, a longer one, between Pentecost and the start of Advent. How long each is, depends on when Easter is. If Easter is very early then there is hardly any Ordinary Time before Lent and there is, consequently, a very long time of Ordinary Time between Pentecost and Advent. In those churches which use lectionaries, I often hear people sigh with slight despondency about 'Ordinary Time', especially during the long period that stretches across the summer months. It can feel a little as though we are faced with a long stretch of not very much; a slightly bland, unexciting series of Sundays with little particular focus or indeed much to recommend them.

There is a certain irony in the recognition that the term 'Ordinary Time' is not a historic one but comes from the liturgical revisions of Vatican Two in 1969. So the churches began calling thirty-three or thirty-four weeks of the year 'ordinary' just at the time when ordinariness was beginning to go out of fashion and was replaced by an increasing emphasis on the new and exciting. We should note, however, that the meaning of the word 'ordinary' in this instance is not 'commonplace or everyday' but 'measured'. The Latin term *tempus ordinarium* from which we get the English term 'Ordinary Time' means literally measured time and refers to the numbering of the weeks through a given period of time: 'the first Sunday after ... the second Sunday after' ... and so on.

In step with the rhythms of life

Ordinary Time has within it an expectation of rhythm, of the measured passing of time. This implies that Ordinary Time is not just to be endured or ignored while it slips dully away but to be noted, noticed and numbered. The rhythmic marking of the first week, second week, third week and so on, allows us not just to let time slip through our fingers but to remember it, to cherish it and to mark the span from the previous week to the following week. It is so easy with all the pressures of everyday life to let hours slip into days, days into weeks, and weeks into months, until years if not decades have passed while we barely notice.

A commitment to Ordinary Time, then, is a commitment to time itself, to the marking off of days and weeks, not so that we can wish them away but so that we can savour them. Ordinary Time challenges us to become 'measured people', people who commit themselves to a greater spaciousness of living and to a less frenetic mode of being. It invites us to be more generous to ourselves and to re-interrogate the rhythms of our life to ensure that our ordinary lives contain enough space within them for us to flourish.

As we mark week after week, we are challenged to celebrate the good times and grieve for the bad, to recall our joys and confess our failings. This rhythmic passing of time is one which the monastic tradition understands profoundly. The monastic life of regular prayer and worship, often in places of outstanding natural beauty is, as Esther de Waal notes in her book *The Spiritual Journey*, designed to help anyone 'become more conscious of the sacredness of time and place' (E. de Waal, *The Spiritual Journey*, St Bede's Publications, 1993, p. 49). In other words the monastic life draws people deeply into ordinariness though the passing of time in a particular place and it is in that ordinariness that they encounter God.

Many people today are beginning to rediscover the value of monastic living, whether through its traditional forms or through 'new monasticism' which seeks to use the insights of the monastic tradition both in modern day communities and in everyday life. One of the aims of new monasticism is to take the principles of monastic living and to make it applicable to modern life. Even so the particular principles that arise in monasticism are not for everyone. The challenge for each one of us is to find a rhythm that works with our personality, our home life and our working pattern.

One of the complexities of this is that, when you have found the rhythm that works for you and you have done it for long enough, then the rhythm carries you. I have often heard the people who say Morning and Evening prayer regularly, reflect on the fact that no matter how bad your day is, how unprepared for worship you are, how distracted you are by the many competing demands of life, the service itself carries you along. It is a little like steering into the current of a river. Once there the rhythm does the rest, pulling you closer and deeper into the presence of God. The problem is getting into the rhythm in the first place. It takes discipline, practice and sometimes pure grim determination to get over the hump of boredom, distraction and busyness into the rhythm beyond.

Finding the rhythm of your own soul

For some, saying some form of daily office allows them easy access to the deep rhythm of the soul. There are a wide number to choose from, ranging from those that have arisen from particular monastic communities like *Celebrating Common Prayer* from the Anglican Franciscans

(Continuum, 2003), or *Celtic Daily Prayer* from the Northumbrian Community (Collins, 2005) to those that are more denominationally focused like the Church of England's Morning, Evening or Mid-Day prayer (now available online and in a beautifully produced soft leather binding called *Time to Pray*) or the Jesuit podcast *Pray as you Go*, which can be downloaded to an IPod or MP3 player.

For others the rhythm takes the form of daily Bible study (with or without notes), or weekly prayer groups or Bible studies, or meditation alone or in a group. The list could go on and on. The form that the rhythm could take is almost limitless, the challenge that we each face is simply finding out what the rhythm of our own soul is at any one point in our life.

I learnt this lesson (again!) when my children were smaller. The two most influential rhythms in my spiritual life before I had children were daily reading of the Bible (or to be more honest aiming for daily and hitting a few times a week) and the saying of Morning or Evening prayer. Both of these went out of the window when I had children. Neither fitted easily into my life and I got to the stage of assuming that I had to give up on spirituality for a while until the children grew up.

If I'm honest this wasn't a new struggle, simply a new form of the old one. I've always struggled with praying. The problem is that I'm an extrovert. My best thoughts come when other people are around. I think out loud. I'm closest to God when I'm doing something with my hands. Over the years people have suggested to me that I go on silent retreat to deepen my spirituality. I've learnt through bitter experience that this is a path of unremitting torture. When I do go on silent retreat, I get depressed and obsessed with my own inability to pray alone. Rather than bringing me closer to God it alienates me from myself ... and so I've given up trying. I deeply respect – still even envy – those who can pray alone for hours on end, who enjoy silent retreats and need time by themselves to be with God but have given up beating myself up (most of the time at any rate) about the fact that I can't do it myself.

Given this aspect of my personality and the stage that we had reached in our family life, it is hardly surprising that all sense of rhythm, prayer and spirituality went down the tubes until I realized that I was looking at it the wrong way around. Instead, with the help of a wise and wonderful friend, I began to work out what my own deep rhythms were, or to put it another way where I felt closest to God. Very much to my surprise, I discovered that I did have my own deep rhythms; they were just not what I thought they should be. The time when God draws closest in my life is ordinary times: when I'm spending time with my family; when I'm digging, planting and harvesting on the allotment; when I'm making things; when I'm reading and writing. My life, I discovered, was packed with deep rhythms of the soul, I just hadn't allowed them to be counted as such.

Without these times my life grows thin and my inner reservoir runs dry. The challenge for me is to make these my 'ordinary time', the measured, rhythm of life in which I expect to – and often do – meet God. These are the places in the river to which I must learn to return again and again, until the undercurrent lifts me up and draws me along. They are my 'ordinary time' but that does not mean that they will be – or indeed should be – everyone's. Many Christians need silence and aloneness, just as I need noise and company. The key is to find what yours is, and then to find its rhythm.

This also does not mean I never read the Bible (I am a writer and lecturer in the Bible after all!), nor that I don't relish church services, but that for now, for me, at this particular stage of my life my rhythm of prayer takes an unusual but rich expression. I have no doubt that it will change in the future, and when it does I will almost certainly need to learn the lesson all over again, but for now I have a rhythm that works (except for when it doesn't).

Everyday God

As I reflected on my slow realization about where my own particular rhythm is to be found, I have been intrigued by my own assumptions. I think I assumed that I couldn't be praying when digging or playing or cooking because it wasn't 'sacred' enough, not sufficiently set apart to be holy. This seems to be implied in the following quote from Joni Eareckson Tada's book *Heaven: Your Real Home* (Zondervan, 1995):

> Few are skilled at holding themselves in a state of listening to heaven's music. Ordinary Things – like kitchen pots clattering, telephones ringing and TV commercials about frozen food and dishwashing detergent – drown out the song.

While I know what she is saying here, I disagree with how she expresses it. For me, the point is that heaven's song sings just as vibrantly in and through the kitchen pots clattering and the telephones ringing but, like R. S. Thomas observed in 'The Bright Field', we go on our way looking for something else, or, as I did, we assume that heaven's song cannot be found there and so look elsewhere. Our natural instinct follows that of Peter on the mountain of transfiguration who wanted to build 'special' dwellings for Jesus, Moses and Elijah to mark the importance of the event. We want to preserve the moment, set it apart and make it holy. To do this we build fine buildings, paint exquisite art, sing powerful and stirring music and go aside from our daily lives into silence and contemplation or Bible study and prayer groups. All of this is the proper response to an encounter with the one who created the world, who sits in splendour upon a heavenly throne, who has redeemed the world and will come again in glory. It is a good instinct in that it recognizes the sacredness of our encounters with God and sets apart times and spaces in which we can remind ourselves of God's extraordinariness. However, we need to guard against the assumption that God can only be found in sacred spaces and at sacred times.

The God who was properly worshipped in the majesty and wonder of the temple in Israel, was also the God who yearned for humble, contrite hearts. As Isaiah 57.17 reminds us, God dwells in the lofty places and with those ordinary, everyday people who respond to him genuinely. The God whose temple was gilded with gold, was also the God who cherished the two small copper coins of the widow in Luke 21.1–4. The God whose throne is in heaven, is also the God whose son was laid in a feeding trough and who lived in the hill country of Galilee. God is indeed a Sunday (or Saturday) best God but he is also an everyday God and is as much to be found with those washing up as with those in grand cathedrals, as much in mud pies as in gold and silver vessels, as much in the ordinary things of life as in the special, sacred things.

This is something we all know intellectually but struggle to put into practice. Somehow it's easier to expect to encounter God in splendour than in squalor; though in reality, if, as the biblical tradition reminds us, it is not God who prefers the splendour, we might need to ask ourselves why we are so keen to ensure that God is set apart in glory and majesty.

Everyday Christians

The reason why it is so important to recapture our sense of the ordinary is twofold. First, as I reflected above, if we insist in keeping God in splendour we lose so many opportunities to encounter him in our everyday lives. If we wait for silence, for fine surroundings, for spectacular music or art, then we devastate our chances of encountering the everyday God who stands by patiently illuminating the fields of our lives, while we pass by without noticing. The second reason is as important as the first. If we insist on God being 'Sunday best'; then we naturally assume we have to be too.

I remember, as a child, listening with wide eyes to the spectacular stories and testimonies of those whose lives had been transformed by their Christian faith. Oddly, however, I never found this encouraging for my own faith, since I knew that my story would never be as dramatic as theirs. It took me years to realize that the fact that I had been brought up Christian and could only recount the gentle companionship of God over years rather than a dramatic account of transformation did not make me an inadequate Christian. Mine is not a dramatic story of faith – more an everyday one – but my ordinary, unexciting story of faith is as valued by God as the spectacular ones.

We do not need to be celebrity Christians, with fantastic, dramatic stories of faith. Our everyday God cherishes everyday Christians. What we need to learn to do, however, is to become better at telling our stories of everyday faith. This returns us to the theme of how important it is that we have confidence in ordinariness. We have become enculturated by the assumption that no story is worth telling unless it is dramatic, exciting and unusual, and so we no longer tell the ordinary stories. Because we do not tell the ordinary stories, we give the implicit message that everyday faith is of less value than dramatic, life changing experiences. The solution, of course, is to learn to tell our ordinary stories of faith with more confidence and in doing so we may discover that those moments of the sunbeams breaking through, that R. S. Thomas talks about, become more easily noticeable as we train ourselves to become recognizers of the extraordinary, ordinary things of God.

On balance

Of course the problem with all this is that it can feel a little like counsel in favour of laziness: don't bother to set aside time for silence, you can worship God just as well at home as at church and there is no need to grow up into deeper and more profound faith – God loves you just as you are. All of these are true *and* false both at the same time. You don't need to lay aside time for silence, God is as much present in the hustle and bustle of everyday life as in the silence and tranquillity of prayer, but if we never lay aside time for silence, our inner ear will became less attuned to the still, small voice of God and we will find it harder to hear him in the hustle and bustle. You can worship God at home but unless we make corporate worship an important part of our lives, our daily worship of God can become shallow and thin. God does love you just the way you are but yearns that we all become the fullest and most Christ-like human being that we can.

The point about ordinariness is that it is the proper balance to extraordinariness. Our lives need both. The rhythm of the ordinary helps us to understand and celebrate more fully the festival times like Christmas and Easter; and those festival times help us to identify the things of God in ordinary times. God is to be found in the daily grind of life but it is taking time out of that grind in praise and prayer that helps us to recognize God in the ordinary things of life. God calls us just as we are, ordinary, everyday Christians, and summons us onwards into extraordinariness. We need both the everyday and the special, the ordinary and the extraordinary, and we need to wrestle to keep them in balance. Too much ordinary and we can lose sight of God; too much extraordinary and we slip into assuming that God, like us, does not really cherish the everyday.

This book seeks to celebrate ordinary faith and life in all its forms and as it does so to weave the extraordinary into the ordinary: to recognize that ordinary people, no matter who they are and what they do, are all extraordinary; to celebrate the fact that the extraordinary God we worship is most likely to be found among the ordinary things of life; and to remind us that glimpses of God or glimmers of glory are most likely to be found when, in the words of R. S. Thomas, we turn aside at nothing more extraordinary than a small field, 'to a brightness that seemed as transitory as your youth once, but is the eternity that awaits you'.

PART ONE

Ordinary People

I

ON TURNING ASIDE

One of the characteristics that allows someone in the midst of an ordinary, everyday existence to encounter God is their ability to turn aside from what they are doing and to notice the daisy or the rainbow or the burning bush in the midst of the mundane. I often wonder, however, what might have happened if Moses had not turned aside at the burning bush. What if, at the crucial moment a sheep had fallen dangerously and needed rescuing so that he didn't notice that the bush was burning, or what if he did notice but it was a meal time and he thought he might investigate at a more convenient moment, or what if he decided it wasn't that spectacular after all and not worth turning aside to see? Of course we cannot know, because it didn't happen. No more than we can know what might have happened if we had turned aside, on those countless moments when the sunbeam broke through, when the daisy mirrored heaven, when someone was ready to talk, and we didn't notice. Our lives are peppered with myriad potential 'what ifs'. What if we had done this, not that? What if we hadn't done that?

Living a faithful ordinary life is not about torturing ourselves with the endless 'what ifs', so much as it is about focusing ourselves on the 'what might bes'. If Moses had missed the moment and not turned aside, he might well have missed his encounter with God at the burning bush, but there would have been other encounters, other times when God broke through and spoke. Reflecting on what we might have missed could so easily become an exercise in regret, in living out our lives in wistful longing for what could have been if only … instead, the calling to faithful, ordinary living is about reflecting on what we might have missed, so that we don't miss it again; so that the next time the occasion arises we are primed and ready to go.

Part of this is simply training ourselves to be the kind of people who *do* turn aside. People who are not so fixed on the path we tread that our curiosity cannot be piqued so that we turn off and meet something new. People whose horizons stretch beyond the grind of life's rat-run, who simply look up from time to time, and see the bush burning, or the sunbeam breaking through. People who when they see these things recognize them for the potential they offer and who turn aside in the hope of an encounter with God. Turning aside is the most ordinary of actions but can have the most extraordinary of consequences, as Moses discovered.

❦

1 On curiosity and taking time

Exodus 3.1–3 Moses was keeping the flock of his father-in-law Jethro, the priest of Midian; he led his flock beyond the wilderness, and came to Horeb, the mountain of God. There the angel of the LORD appeared to him in a flame of fire out of a bush; he looked, and the bush was blazing, yet it was not consumed. Then Moses said, 'I must turn aside and look at this great sight, and see why the bush is not burned up.'

For further reading: Exodus 3.1–6

It all started when he turned aside. Moses, it appeared, had been contentedly looking after his father-in-law's sheep since he fled Egypt years before. His extraordinary existence in the Pharaoh's palace had been replaced with an ordinary existence, shaped by little more remarkable than finding the next grazing patch for his father-in-law's sheep. But when he turned aside, his life turned upside down. Of course, we can't help wondering whether he arrived by accident at Mount Horeb, the mountain of God, or whether he had set his path towards Mount Horeb in the hope that he might encounter God. As with so many of the biblical stories, we are left with as many questions as answers, but whatever he intended when he brought his flock close to Mount Horeb, it was Moses' willingness to turn aside when he saw the bush burning which transformed his life.

The Hebrew word, translated 'turn aside', even more than its English translation has the sense of stepping off a pre-determined path and it is this that seems so important in this story. It was Moses' willingness to change his plan and to step off the path that he was following for this whole event to happen. In this instance, Moses' predetermined path was finding the next patch of grass for his father-in-law's sheep. In our high-octane, high-performance culture this may seem a benign, gently pastoral way of life. In reality it was the opposite. Grazing sheep in what is effectively desert territory is a desperate task, with no guarantees of success. Add to this the wild animals who would stalk the flock ready to pluck off a sheep should the shepherd's attention be caught for a moment and Moses' life begins to feel much more pressured and urgent. For him turning aside could have meant the loss of one or more of his father-in-law's sheep.

In comparison our inability to turn aside may feel a little feeble, though nonetheless real. We spend such a lot of our lives trying to keep 'on track' whatever we mean by this. So often my own life involves running constantly from one thing to the to next with my eye so fixed on the next task (for which I'm often late) that I wonder whether I would notice if the equivalent of a burning bush lit up in my life. And if I did notice, would I allow myself the time to turn aside and investigate, or would I, instead mark it down on my to-do list as something to come back and explore more deeply when I've got a minute?

Turning aside seems to require at least two key characteristics: curiosity and the willingness to take time to explore. Curiosity is not often held up as a spiritual virtue. As a child, I was encouraged to mind my own business and instructed not to fiddle. Now I am a parent myself I understand this instruction all too well, but a child's curiosity seems to me to be a vital part of a healthy spirituality. Good answers are, of course, very important for Christian faith but at least as important, if not more so, is the ability to ask good questions. The problem is that many of us, as adults, are simply not curious enough. We've learnt the childhood lesson well and mind our own business – or is that busyness? As a result we no longer explore with either our fingers or our minds.

Moses' inner conversation with himself (which is again more vivid in Hebrew than can be expressed in English and is something along the lines of 'Let me turn aside and ...') suggests a lively curiosity that led him to want to know more. He was intrigued and followed his instinct to see more.

This, of course, is closely connected to the second characteristic needed for turning aside: the willingness to take time to explore. Busyness can so often prevent us from doing something only on the off chance that it might produce something. Before we begin, we want to be assured of results, to be confident that the time we take out will produce fruit and be worth the time we spend on it. The problem is that God isn't like that. God doesn't sign on the dotted line to give guaranteed satisfaction at a pre-selected and pre-determined time before engaging with the world. Instead God gives a hint here, a suggestion there or a glimmer on the horizon. Busy people are all too likely to miss God's presence because we do not have the leisure to follow up the hints, suggestions and glimmers on the off chance that occasionally, like Moses, we might encounter the living God.

Sometimes it all begins when we turn aside – the question is whether we have the curiosity and are prepared to take the time out to do so.

༄

2 And then living with the consequences

Exodus 3.7–11 Then the Lord *said, 'I have observed the misery of my people who are in Egypt; I have heard their cry on account of their taskmasters. Indeed, I know their sufferings, and I have come down to deliver them from the Egyptians, and to bring them up out of that land to a good and broad land, a land flowing with milk and honey, to the country of the Canaanites, the Hittites, the Amorites, the Perizzites, the Hivites, and the Jebusites. The cry of the Israelites has now come to me; I have also seen how the Egyptians oppress them. So come, I will send you to Pharaoh to bring my people, the Israelites, out of Egypt.' But Moses said ...*

For further reading: Exodus 3.7 – 4.13

Any encounter with God should come with a health warning. Encounters with God are accompanied with life-changing consequences. Moses certainly seemed to regret the consequences of his encounter with God – if not the encounter itself – almost immediately. This is because, as is so often the case with encounters with God, God did not reveal himself to Moses simply so that Moses could enjoy the encounter, or so that he could feel better about his spiritual journey, but so that Moses could do what God asked him to.

One of the features that interests me about modern discussions about spirituality and mysticism is that sometimes – often even – what we might call religious experiences are perceived as being for their own sake: to help us along in our spiritual journey or to teach us more about God. It is hard, however, to think of any encounter with God in the Old or New Testaments that is not accompanied with the command to do something: Elijah's encounter with 'the still small voice' on Mount Horeb sent him to anoint new kings; Isaiah's great vision in the temple in Isaiah 6 comes with the command to proclaim God's word to a people who would not listen; Ezekiel's vision of God's chariot in Ezekiel 1 set the scene for Ezekiel being sent as prophet to the people in Exile. For many people today the purpose of encountering God is their own spiritual journey; for the biblical writers the purpose of encountering God is mission, by which I mean being sent out to do God's will in the world. People who have a lively spiritual life should expect to have a correspondingly lively life of mission in the world; you can't have one without the other. Moses discovered this to his cost. What began as turning aside out of curiosity, ended as being sent on the most challenging mission conceivable: to free God's people from slavery.

It is easy to believe that great biblical heroes are somehow more prepared for God's call than we are; that where we stumble, hesitate and procrastinate, they leap in with guts and enthusiasm. In all honesty we can only believe this if we don't read the texts too carefully. The biblical heroes are easily as reluctant as we are to be involved with God's mission in the world and none more so than Moses. The opening of verse 11, 'But Moses said ...', opens up a section in which Moses objects to God's call. He begins by asking who he is to be called to this: 'Who am I that I should go to Pharaoh, and bring the Israelites out of Egypt?' Exodus 3.11; moving swiftly on to who he should say God is: 'If I come to the Israelites and say to them, "The God of your ancestors has sent me to you," and they ask me, "What is his name?" what shall I say to them?' 3.13. From there Moses looks at worst case scenarios: 'But suppose they do not believe me or listen to me' 4.1; and his own inabilities: 'O my Lord, I have never been eloquent, neither in the past nor even now that you have spoken to your servant; but I am slow of speech and slow of tongue' 4.10. Finally he gets to his real point: 'O my Lord, please send someone else' 4.13.

The point is that although to us Moses is a great leader, to him he was simply an ordinary person about his ordinary life who was suddenly called to something so extraordinary that he found it hard to comprehend it. What we notice in Moses' grand argument with God about why he really shouldn't have chosen him for the task, is God's infinite patience and reassurance. Over and over again, God assures Moses that he will be with him to provide all the extraordinary features that are needed. God makes clear in the face of Moses' objections that he doesn't need to be well known or a brilliant theologian able to describe in detail who God is. He doesn't need to be an optimist believing that it will all go well, or a good communicator. He doesn't even need, it appears, to be all that willing. All God expects is that Moses goes to do what God requests. God still calls us as we are to provide the ordinary to his extraordinary and is still, I imagine, as frustrated by our attempts to point to all the people who would be better at it than we would be. God still calls us in all our ordinariness, all we have to do is go ... when we do we discover that God's promise to Moses remains and that, wherever we go, he is with us.

♥ʒʞ♥

3 You cannot be serious!

Jonah 1.1–3 Now the word of the LORD came to Jonah son of Amittai, saying, 'Go at once to Nineveh, that great city, and cry out against it; for their wickedness has come up before me.' But Jonah set out to flee to Tarshish from the presence of the LORD.

For further reading: Jonah 1.4–17 and chapters 3 – 4

One of the glories of deciding to choose to look at the 'ordinary' people of the Bible is the almost unlimited choice that this presents. The Bible is stuffed with stories of ordinary people, doing ordinary things until God breaks in to call them into extraordinariness. So why choose Jonah? Surely he was a prophet already, so not strictly 'ordinary'? I would argue that while his job may not have been ordinary he himself, as a person, was gloriously ordinary, with ordinary responses, reactions and grumbles.

Jonah turned aside but not in the way that Moses did. Jonah's turning aside took an entirely new direction (literally!). Jonah has to be one of the most comic books of the Bible, a comedy that begins even in its first three verses. This is even more vivid in the Hebrew than in English, where the word of the Lord came to Jonah and said, 'Arise, go to Nineveh.' So Jonah arose ... and went to Tarshish. No one is quite clear where Tarshish is but the one thing that scholars are agreed upon is that it is in the opposite direction to Nineveh. Jonah half obeyed God in that he arose and went, the only problem is that he didn't quite go where he was meant to go! Jonah certainly turned aside but this time he turned aside to run in the opposite direction.

It seems as though Jonah is all too aware of the consequences of encountering God, and thought that he would cut these short by eluding God's notice. Again the Hebrew seems to stress this by saying that Jonah went to Tarshish 'away from the face of the Lord'. The implication seems to be that God is looking from Jonah to Nineveh, therefore if Jonah scarpered to Tarshish God might be so busy looking at Nineveh he wouldn't notice that Jonah had gone. Jonah was playing hide and seek with God but one of the many points of this story is that God is not such a local God that you can escape his gaze. Wherever we go, God is there (as the Psalmist who observed in Psalm 139: 'If I ascend to heaven, you are there; if I make my bed in Sheol, you are there'). In other words there is no getting away from God.

The story of Jonah is the antidote to any fear that we might have somehow missed the moment – the one moment – when God wanted to speak to us, to which I referred to at the start of this chapter. There is, in fact, no need to ask the question of what might have happened if I had turned aside at this moment, or had the time to encounter God properly on that occasion. While it is entirely possible that we can and do miss glimmers of God's presence in our world, the people who lose out when we miss these glimmers are ourselves. The story of Jonah is a story that reminds us that God doesn't give up all that easily.

This is a truth that runs as a strand through the many stories of people's calling to ordination that I have heard during twelve years of teaching in theological colleges. Over and over again, I have heard people describing that un-scratchable itch, or that unavoidable sense of calling that eventually and inexorably brings them to the point of ordination. Of course vocations are not just to ordination but to all aspects of our lives: to marriage or singleness; to having or not having children; to the work we do; to the places we live; to the communities we serve; to the churches in which we worship and the various and varying ministries to which we are called.

Whatever our vocation, the one marker of genuineness is that the sense of calling will simply not go away. So if you really want to test a vocation, whatever it is to, then fight it. Fight it with all that you have. Be like Jonah and run as far in the opposite direction as fast as you can – and you can be sure that if your calling is true, God will find you there and draw you back.

Jonah is probably the most reluctant of all reluctant servants of God. He makes Moses' response to God at the burning bush look positively enthusiastic. One of the reasons I love him so much as a character is that he is in my mind a cross between John McEnroe (he who used to throw his tennis racket to the ground while shouting 'you cannot be serious!') and Eeyore, from the Winnie the Pooh stories, who is depressive and never expects anything good anyway. Jonah reminds us powerfully that for some crazy reason, despite the fact that we are often a hindrance rather than a help, God wants to include us in his mission and message of love.

Jonah also reminds us that the success of that mission is more down to God than to us. Jonah was not only reluctant, but cursory (his message was simply: 'Forty days more, and Nineveh shall be overthrown!' Jonah 3.4). He was also grumpy and angry with God when God did in fact forgive the people of Nineveh (Jonah 3.10—4.1). Despite Jonah, however, God's message transformed the people of Nineveh. This does not give us an excuse to be reluctant, cursory and grumpy in our vocations but it does reassure us that God can and does act despite us, as well as through us.

Jonah's turning aside took a very different form to Moses', he was far from a willing participant in God's plan for Nineveh. His responses to God's call are not what you might term exemplary but they are recognizable and understandable. Jonah's response to God is in many ways ordinary – in that he is not the only person to respond so badly to God's call – but despite him and through him the people of Nineveh were, the story tells us, transformed.

☙❦❧

4 Distracted by much ministry?

Luke 10.38–42 Now as they went on their way, he entered a certain village, where a woman named Martha welcomed him into her home. She had a sister named Mary, who sat at the Lord's feet and listened to what he was saying. But Martha was distracted by her many tasks; so she came to him and asked, 'Lord, do you not care that my sister has left me to do all the work by myself? Tell her then to help me.' But the Lord answered her, 'Martha, Martha, you are worried and distracted by many things; there is need of only one thing. Mary has chosen the better part, which will not be taken away from her.'

While we are on the subject of people who are not good at turning aside, we should turn our gaze to Martha. Martha is, on the surface, a perfect example of someone who failed to turn aside from her 'many tasks' to take the time to sit and to listen. The way in which the passage is translated in most of the modern translations suggests a slightly fussy woman who simply can't leave alone her 'many tasks' (New Revised Standard Version) or 'all the serving' (New Jerusalem Bible) or 'all the preparations' (New International Version).

My mental (entirely historically inaccurate) image of her is of a harassed looking middle-aged woman, wearing an apron, with hair descending from an untidy bun. This mental image may or may not have been influenced by the numerous talks and sermons I've heard which seem to assume that Martha's major crime here is that she has an over obsession with housework and wanting everything 'just so'; whereas if she had been more properly in touch with her spirituality she would have been able to stop fussing around her inconsequential tasks and to take time to listen to Jesus. In other words if she had been able to be drawn less into the ordinary things of life and to have taken time out of her humdrum concerns, then she might have been able to encounter and learn from Jesus.

It probably won't come as much of a surprise to anyone to discover that I view this passage somewhat differently. Not because I am a fan of housework– quite the opposite in fact – but because I feel that Martha is often viewed too harshly in interpretations of this story. The first point to notice is that it isn't Martha who is acting unusually, but Mary. The description of Mary sitting at the feet of Jesus is a description that suggests that Mary is adopting the attitude of a disciple to her Rabbi. The disciples of Rabbis gathered around their feet to listen, learn and discuss what they heard. In the world that Mary and

Martha inhabited this would have been shocking and revolutionary, women would have never dreamt of even sitting down in the company of men who were not related to them, let alone sitting in the posture of one who is a disciple.

What Martha missed here was a rare opportunity to overthrow the expectations of her gender and to sit and learn from Jesus. The reason she didn't immediately sit down when Jesus arrived was probably because it never occurred to her that she could. This may have been due to her busyness or it may have been due to cultural norms. Either way the story reminds us that we should not become so bound up with the tasks before us nor indeed with what we know to be the right thing to do, that we miss the revolutionary presence of Jesus gently reminding us that our to-do lists and our etiquette are as nothing compared with the chance of sitting at his feet for a while. As a result of her many preoccupations, Martha risked missing her own extraordinary encounter with Jesus.

So what was she preoccupied with? The answer is almost certainly with preparing food for the sudden influx of guests into their house, and in this the modern translations are correct to render the verse as 'many tasks', 'all the serving' or 'all the preparations'. It is easy to fall into the trap, however, of assuming that where Martha went wrong was that she was concerned with inconsequential tasks. Apart from the fact that the feeding of hungry guests is hugely important (especially in a culture which places as much emphasis on hospitality as first-century Judaism does), this seems to misunderstand what is going on here.

One of the intriguing features of the Greek of this passage is that the word translated as 'tasks' 'serving' or 'preparations' is elsewhere translated as 'ministry' or 'service'. If we were to render this verse as 'Martha was distracted by much ministry', the whole story gains a different perspective. Martha wasn't distracted with irrelevant minutiae so much as with fulfilling her calling; and Martha's 'tasks' were ministry in that she was engaging in those things which were her particular responsibility and to which she had been called. What she was doing was not inconsequential. It was essential, but nevertheless she allowed what she was doing to distract her from the one necessary thing of sitting at Jesus' feet.

Here we encounter a vital distinction between fully engaging in the ordinary tasks to which we are called in the expectation that there we can meet God and between becoming so distracted by those tasks that we risk missing the unexpected encounters God places on our path. It isn't what we do that affects this, but how we do it.

༺✿༻

5 Come and See

John 1.43–46 The next day Jesus decided to go to Galilee. He found Philip and said to him, 'Follow me.' Now Philip was from Bethsaida, the city of Andrew and Peter. Philip found Nathanael and said to him, 'We have found him about whom Moses in the law and also the prophets wrote, Jesus son of Joseph from Nazareth.' Nathanael said to him, 'Can anything good come out of Nazareth?' Philip said to him, 'Come and see.'

For further reading: John 1.35–51

One of the legendary sayings in my family is attributed to my Grandad who is said to have declared in the face of anything new: 'I don't like that, what is it?' In my more irreverent moments I have wondered whether we could work it into church services as a liturgical response to suggestions of change. What it expresses so well is the natural human suspicion of things we don't know, or things that fall outside the parameters of what we are comfortable with or know to be true.

Nathanael's response to Philip in John 1.46 falls very close to this kind of saying. Nathanael knows it to be a self-evident truth that nothing and no one good comes from Nazareth. It is interesting to ask why he might think that. What was so bad about Nazareth? Nathanael's saying trips off his lips, a little like my Grandad's used to trip off his; this is no new prejudice but a well ingrained one. The problem is that it is hard for those of us who know nothing of the basis of Nathanael's dislike to know where it came from. There are two main options. One is that since Nathanael came from Cana (as we discover in John 21.2), a neighbouring village to Nazareth, there might have been a historic enmity between the two. The problem is that if there was, this is the only evidence for it.

A second possibility is that Nazareth, like the whole of Galilee, was seen as an inadequate origin for the Messiah who was thought to come from Judaea, the southern kingdom, and specifically from Bethlehem. It is worth remembering that Galilee in the north had only relatively recently become part of the Jewish nation again. After the northern kingdom fell in 722 BC, the Assyrians mixed up the population and for all intents and purposes the northern kingdom as it had existed before then came to an end, but during the period of the Maccabees (late 2nd century BC) Galilee was brought back into the Jewish nation. As a result Jews from Judaea, which had always been Jewish, regarded Galilee suspiciously and certainly not as the place that the Messiah would come from. Of course the problem with this is that Nathanael was also from Galilee. If this is what he meant there might have been certain sarcasm behind his question.

As with so many of these issues we will probably never know what Nathanael had against Nazareth; the real point of the story is what happened next. Nathanael expressed a view steeped in prejudice (whether that of his own or one that was widely held) and Philip simply responded 'Come and see'. Philip's invitation to Nathanael was to leave behind the track upon which he was set and to look again at what he knew to be true. Of course the outcome was an encounter with Jesus, where Nathanael realized not only that something good could indeed come out of Nazareth but that it had in the person of Jesus.

This passage illustrates that it is not just a lack of curiosity, nor indeed extreme busyness, nor even, as with Jonah, an unwillingness to do what God has asked, that prevents us from turning aside. Sometimes it is prejudice. Or to put it more gently, knowing already that something is the case so that we do not need to investigate further. So often our minds are so firmly set on a certain course that we simply cannot see beyond it. We do not intend to be closed minded, we simply do not expect to find anything good in a certain place, and so we don't. On occasions like this, we need someone like Philip to challenge us to think again, to look beyond what we know to be true and to see it with fresh eyes.

Sometimes turning aside comes naturally but sometimes we need help. Sometimes we need the intervention of someone like Philip who is able to come alongside us and suggest that we might 'come and see' before we decide too firmly that what is over there simply cannot be of God. Indeed the challenge of faithful Christian living is being open to the 'Philips' we meet along the way who invite us to turn aside and to 'come and see'. The 'Philips' we meet along the way may not always be right but if we decide that before going to see, we risk missing an encounter with the one who knows everything about us.

꒰ꔛ꒱

6 Oi! You!

Acts 9.1–5 Meanwhile Saul, still breathing threats and murder against the disciples of the Lord, went to the high priest and asked him for letters to the synagogues at Damascus, so that if he found any who belonged to the Way, men or women, he might bring them bound to Jerusalem. Now as he was going along and approaching Damascus, suddenly a light from heaven flashed around him. He fell to the ground and heard a voice saying to him, 'Saul, Saul, why do you persecute me?' He asked, 'Who are you, Lord?' The reply came, 'I am Jesus, whom you are persecuting.'

For further reading: Acts 9.1–22

As a parent, I have learnt a lot about repeating myself. The conversation often goes: 'Mum, can I have …' (fill in the blank as appropriate) to which I sometimes – though not always – reply: 'No.' Five minutes later the request comes again: 'Mum, can I have …' or if they are working together as a team, my other daughter will come: 'Mum, can I have …' On a bad day this goes on and on, until I pop and the shouting starts, to which my daughters give the affronted and slightly outraged response: 'I only asked.' Sometimes in the Bible we get a glimpse of the moment when God's shouting begins. The case of Paul on the road to Damascus is, of course, an example not of God being asked something but asking. Here God attempts to catch Paul's attention, so that he can realize who Jesus of Nazareth really was and then be sent out to proclaim it to the ends of the earth.

I often wonder whether Paul's experience on the road to Damascus is the first time that God has addressed Paul, or whether it was the culmination of a long series of attempts to speak to him which eventually ends in shouting. It is possible that this is the first time God spoke to Paul and, knowing what kind of person he was, decided that it was only the loud, shouting approach that could break through into Paul's consciousness, with the divine equivalent of 'Oi! You!' Either way, God certainly grabbed Paul's attention, this time.

It would have been hard not to with such a dramatic intervention. Here again, as in the case of Jonah, God demonstrates that when necessary, when we have been avoiding the burning bush moment for long enough, God can and will break in dramatically, so that there can be no doubt at all about what is meant. Most of us are much more subtle than Jonah in avoiding God's call. We don't board a ship and sail to the furthest ocean; we simply – and often politely – look in the opposite direction. In all fairness the reason for this is often not deliberate but simply because we aren't sure that we did in fact hear God's voice. One of the most common conversations I have with people about where God wants them to go next is framed around the question of 'How do I know what God wants?' Quite frankly a few burning bushes, flashing lights and booming voices would come in handy from time to time as we seek to work out what God wants of us.

One answer to this conundrum is to become very, very good at looking out for God. One of my favourite examples of this is of Simeon and Anna in the temple just after

Jesus was born (Luke 2.21–38). Simeon and Anna were people who watched for God's redemption. The somewhat old-fashioned word for this is 'sentinel', which was a soldier whose duty was to keep watch. Simeon and Anna, Luke tells us, were expert Sentinels and had spent many hours watching out for the coming of God's redemption. Simeon was 'righteous and devout, looking forward to the consolation of Israel' (2.25); Anna had spent many, many years fasting and praying in the temple. The result is that even when God appeared in the most unexpected guise (that of an eight-day-old baby) they were able to recognize him and to give thanks for him. How did they do it? The answer is of course practice. Simeon and Anna had spent such a lot of time patiently waiting for signs of God that they recognized them as soon as they appeared.

We have two ends of the spectrum here. What you might call the easy way and the hard way. The easy way is to become so attuned to the things of God in the world around us that we rarely miss any signs of God's presence. The harder way is to wait for the divine, 'Oi! You!'; for that moment when, as Paul experienced it, God's call becomes so unavoidable that there is only one response. For all those people who worry about whether they might have accidentally overlooked God's call, the example of Paul comes as great reassurance. God can, did and does shout when necessary. Paul could, of course, have still taken no notice and gone on his way as before, as can we, but if God is really calling then we can be in no doubt at all that eventually we will know about it.

❧

God calls. The few examples we have looked at in this chapter remind us that God calls ordinary people, in their ordinary lives, with their ordinary skills and abilities, to act extraordinarily for him. The one thing of which we can be certain is that God does call – is calling in fact; what it less certain is whether we will notice and, having noticed, whether we will find the time and courage to turn aside and listen.

It is so easy to assume that God's calling is for someone else – someone less ordinary than me; the reality is that God seems to like ordinary people, since it isn't what they did do that is important but what they will do. As I said earlier in this chapter, God's calling isn't just, or even primarily, about ordained ministry; it isn't even about the Church. It is about living out our lives in fulfillment of what God wants to happen in the world.

You can be sure, therefore, that God is calling you to something; the only question is, to what? Is it to live more responsibly day by day or to travel the globe caring for those who suffer when we don't? Is it to a deeper and more fulfilling community where you live or to up sticks and follow wherever he leads? It is worth noting that callings come at different times throughout our lives. We cannot rest on our laurels and point to that time last year (or even 10, 20, 30 years ago) when we heard God's call and turned aside. Sometimes God's call is to a life transformed (like Paul), or to a lifetime's task (like Moses and Paul), but sometimes it is to a specific, one-off task (like Jonah) or even to a momentary opportunity for learning (like Martha). God is calling all of us all of the time. The challenge we face is whether we have sufficient curiosity, time and courage to turn aside and listen to what he has to say.

The theme that has tied these accounts of differing callings together is the theme of successful or unsuccessful turning aside. What each one of us needs to find is our own method of turning aside. Giving a 'prescription' of how to do it would be to miss the point. The ability to turn aside is more to do with mental attitude than with physical practice. Being the kind of person who notices the sunbeam on the field is about cultivating a frame of mind. Anna and Simeon had it; Jonah did not. Mary had it; Martha did not. Eventually Paul had it but it took a bright light and a voice from heaven for him to get it. For some the cultivation of such a frame of mind will arise from hours of prayer, for others it will involve nothing more than an inner shift so that they view the world differently. The key thing is not how you do it but whether you do it at all.

2

UNSUNG HEROES

So what exactly is an 'ordinary' person? I tried out a few definitions before I realized that there is no such thing. The problem was that every definition I came up with simply didn't fit the people I then went on to talk about. I came to the conclusion that people can only be termed 'ordinary' when seen as a large group from a distance. Indeed the derogatory terms for ordinary people are all plural: hoi polloi (which is from Greek and means simply 'the many'), the lumpy proletariat, or the more modern phrase 'chavs' all refer to people as a group. When you get close and learn something of an individual they stop being ordinary.

So none of the people in the chapter that follows is ordinary. Each character is extraordinary sometimes by virtue of their background, sometimes by virtue of their subsequent influence but always because of what they did. Each one lived their life in the circumstances given to them and, when the moment arose, behaved extraordinarily. A good number of them might have described themselves as ordinary but, as the narrative reveals, none of them really were.

The people of this chapter may not be ordinary but they are the unsung heroes of the Bible; the people whom many of us might struggle to identify or name. People who were all but unknown both before and after they feature in a biblical narrative but who, nevertheless, live out God's call to the best of their capacity, doing what they can in the circumstances.

One of my favourite family films of the past few years is *Mr Magorium's Wonder Emporium* (2007). It's a wonderful film, set in a magical toy shop, about the recovery of confidence, belief and hope. In one scene Mr Magorium talks to his shop assistant (who has lost faith in herself) about life and says memorably, 'Your life is an occasion, rise to it.' Each one of the characters in this chapter has done exactly this. They have risen to the occasion of their lives and their example encourages us to do the same.

⹂⹂⹂

1 You will wear yourself out!

Exodus 18.13–18 The next day Moses sat as judge for the people, while the people stood around him from morning until evening. When Moses' father-in-law saw all that he was doing for the people, he said, 'What is this that you are doing for the people? Why do you sit alone, while all the people stand around you from morning until evening?' Moses said to his father-in-law, 'Because the people come to me to inquire of God. When they have a dispute, they come to me and I decide between one person and another, and I make known to them the statutes and instructions of God.' Moses' father-in-law said to him, 'What you are doing is not good. You will surely wear yourself out, both you and these people with you. For the task is too heavy for you; you cannot do it alone.'

For further reading: Exodus 18.1–27

Some passages from the Bible feel very old and a bit irrelevant, but others jump off the page with a vibrant freshness that makes it feel as though the very same situation could happen today. This exchange between Moses and his relatively unknown father-in-law, Jethro, feels like one of the latter. Jethro is an intriguing character. He is a priest of Midian (though what this entails is never spelt out) and evidently an owner of flocks because Moses is caring for them when he saw the burning bush. He is one of those characters that melts in and out of the story and from this moment onwards never reappears in the narrative.

One of the great diseases of our modern society is workaholism: the idea that one's self-worth can be delineated and defined not just by what we do but by how much of it we do. The adage 'less is more' is rarely these days applied to working hours. Instead 'most is best' would sum up current trends much more accurately. This is not to say that every individual believes this. I know many, many people – both women and men – who dearly wish they could work less but the pressures of the working environment mitigate against this, driving them to longer and longer hours.

I would love to contrast the prevailing attitude with those whose working life exists in Christian organizations, like Churches for example. I would love to draw this contrast but, of course, it is impossible to do. Workaholism is just as alive and kicking inside Christian organizations as outside them. Indeed you can be forgiven in some Christian contexts for believing that you have stumbled into the local chapter of a notional workaholics anonymous group, as people apparently vie for the position of busiest and most in demand person present. I hope you understand that the reason I recognize all of this is not because I am not like this but because I am. I too fill my diary and then cram more on top for good measure.

Given this, I can't decide if it is encouraging or depressing to realize that this is not a new problem but one, if not as old as the hills, certainly as old as the people of God. Moses' first steps into leadership were relatively straightforward (if freeing God's people from a despotic tyrant can ever be seen to be straightforward). His early leadership was marked by leading so that others could follow. The story in Exodus 18.13–18 marks the start of the next more complex stage of leadership: governing the day-to-day lives of the Israelites. This is where it seems to begin to go wrong. Moses seems to have assumed that because he, and he alone, was called to lead the people out of Egypt; he and he alone must govern their day-to-day concerns and worries. In other words he fell into the trap of believing himself indispensable and irreplaceable.

In Stef Penney's striking novel *The Tenderness of Wolves,* the main character speaks of her time in a mental asylum where she met someone who believed that he had been called by God to create the perfect steam engine. It would, he believed, save the world from sin. He used up all his money and strength on it and eventually was discovered to be mad. Mrs Ross, the main character, comments about him: 'He knew how important he was in the scheme of things, and would seize each of us in the grounds and beg us to help him escape, so he could continue his vital work. Among those tortured souls, almost all of them bewailing some private anguish, his beseechings were the most heartbreaking I ever heard ... Such is the torment of knowing your own significance' (p. 194).

Moses, in this narrative, had come to know his own significance and so, as Jethro observed, what he was doing was not good because he was wearing himself and the people out. What we miss when we work too hard, is the fact that what begins as good quickly becomes destructive not only of ourselves but also of the people that we are trying to care for. Whether this be on a large scale (such as Moses and the whole people of God) or on the small scale of our own friends and family, most is not best. Most is corrosive of our best selves and best endeavours. What we all need is someone like Jethro who can come and say 'you will surely wear yourself out', now stop and find a better way of doing this.

⊷⋇⊶

2 Live how much you love me

Ruth 1.16–17 But Ruth said, 'Do not press me to leave you or to turn back from following you! Where you go, I will go; where you lodge, I will lodge; your people shall be my people, and your God my God. Where you die, I will die – there will I be buried. May the LORD do thus and so to me, and more as well, if even death parts me from you!'

For further reading: Ruth 1 — 4 (i.e. the whole book – it really is worth the time!)

All families have their small rituals of declaring love. The children's book 'Guess how much I love you' by Sam McBratney recognizes this ritual and illustrates it beautifully. The story features the exchange between a small nut brown hare and a large one who vie to outdo each other in declarations of love beginning with arms stretched out as far as they can go, moving on to how high they can jump and ending with the distance to the moon and back. Having spent many hours reading this book to my daughters (one of whom is called Ruth), I often reflect on the similarities and differences between the two stories. The story of Ruth is a story which needs no arm waving, no jumping up and down and no imaginative analogies. Ruth's love simply flows onwards and outwards from this first declaration of loyalty to Naomi in 1.16–17 to the very end of the story when she gives her her first-born son so that Naomi can have a family of her own again.

The point is that Naomi never has to guess how much Ruth loves her, Ruth shows it in every fibre of her body, in every self-sacrificial act in which she seeks Naomi's welfare. One of the most important moments of this story comes after Ruth has laid down at Boaz's feet and Boaz recognizes the extent of Ruth's loving sacrifice, because then he says to Ruth: 'May you be blessed by the Lord, my daughter; this last instance of your loyalty is better than the first' (Ruth 3.10). In Hebrew this declaration is even more significant than the NRSV implies. The word that Boaz attributes to Ruth's actions here is not just loyalty but the Hebrew word '*ḥesed*', which is very difficult to translate into English. The closest is probably steadfast love.

The importance of the word is that it is the word that sums up the covenant relationship between God and God's people. Loyal, steadfast love in adverse circumstances lies at the heart of the covenant. God never left the people to guess how much he loved them, he showed them again, and again and again. The idea of the covenant is that just as God demonstrates his *ḥesed* so he expects the people to respond and match it with their own. Part of the focus of the narrative of the Old Testament is the illustration of how time and time again the people failed to show their *ḥesed* to God and to their neighbours.

In the context of this Boaz's exclamation to Ruth becomes even more important. Ruth shows the *ḥesed* that the people of God failed to show. What makes this even more remarkable is, of course, that Ruth is not only a woman but a Moabite. The Moabites were ancient enemies of God's people. They lived on the south west border of Israel and fought many battles with Israel. They also profited from Israel's misfortunes as they would swoop in and loot when Israel had been defeated by other enemies. A Moabite woman, therefore, would be regarded as the lowest of the low (a bit like the Samaritan in Jesus' parable of Luke 10.25–37) and yet she lived out *ḥesed* in the way that God's people never managed to do.

The book of Ruth is the ultimate love story. Of course, not a love story as our modern world would render it – a man and woman meeting and finding their emotions transformed into love – but a love story nevertheless. One of the most interesting differences between our modern discussions of love and the portrayals of love in places like the book of Ruth is that our modern discussions of love are about emotion, whereas Ruth's love is about action. Love in the Old and New Testaments is much more about what you do than it is about what you feel. Ruth has *ḥesed* not because she talks about her emotion of love towards Naomi but because the whole of her life is lived out in expression of that love.

I suspect that the story 'Guess how much I love you' would be entirely bemusing in Ruth's world. If you have to guess then it isn't really love. Love is something you see and live out; not something hidden inside. In the end the whole point of the book of Ruth is something of a challenge to all of us. If someone like Ruth, an outsider who has not known God's love, can live out such a remarkable expression of love, how much more must we live love in everything that we do.

3 On doing what you can

2 Samuel 21.8–10 The king took the two sons of Riz-
pah daughter of Aiah, whom she bore to Saul, Armoni
and Mephibosheth; and the five sons of Merab daugh-
ter of Saul, whom she bore to Adriel son of Barzillai
the Meholathite; he gave them into the hands of the
Gibeonites, and they impaled them on the mountain
before the LORD. *The seven of them perished together.*
They were put to death in the first days of harvest,
at the beginning of barley harvest. Then Rizpah the
daughter of Aiah took sackcloth, and spread it on a
rock for herself, from the beginning of harvest until
rain fell on them from the heavens; she did not allow
the birds of the air to come on the bodies by day, or the
wild animals by night.

For further reading: **2 Samuel 21.1–14**
It might also be useful to read **Joshua 9.1–27** *for the*
sake of the back story

One of my all-time favourite stories from the Old Testament must be the story of Rizpah. Rizpah most certainly
falls into the category of unsung heroes of the Bible –
many people have never even heard of her. Even if they
have, the story of what happened to her and how she
responded is embedded in a tale of such gruesomeness
that it is easy to be distracted by that and not to notice
her impact. The story itself is even a little bit hidden, since
it is not in the main bit of the story about David. At the
end of 2 Samuel are a number of stories that were too
important to lose but which didn't fit in the main sweep
of the story and so are gathered together at the end, as a
miscellany or a junk shop of hidden gems.

The reason why I love this story so much is because it seems to respond to that overwhelming emotion that can easily trap us all; the sense that there is nothing that I could do to change what is happening around me so I won't even try. By rights Rizpah should have felt this. When David came to the throne, the Gibeonites asked for revenge because Saul had been wreaking revenge on them. David allowed himself to be persuaded by them and took seven of Saul's sons (two of whom were also Rizpah's sons) and handed them over to the Gibeonites. They, the Gibeonites, murdered them gruesomely on top of the mountain of the Lord. Rizpah was powerless in the face of this and would have been entirely forgiven for staying at home and grieving her sons in private but instead she mourned them publically in such a way that David eventually heard of her grieving protest.

Rizpah's actions were bold and deeply courageous in a way that the face of the story simply doesn't quite communicate: 2 Samuel says that Rizpah stayed by the bodies of her sons and Saul's other sons from the barley harvest until the rains fell. This is a period of about six months: Passover takes place at the time of the barley harvest (so sometime in March or April) and in Israel the rains begin to fall in October. So Rizpah sat there alone, on the top of a mountain for six months beating off vultures and lions, while she sat out her lonely, grieving vigil.

As a result of doing this, two significant things happened. Rizpah's actions stopped a blood feud that had been rumbling for years and persuaded King David to bury his dear friend Jonathan. The blood feud stretched all the way back to the time that the people of God settled in the land. Joshua 9 tells the story of how the Gibeonites (called there the Hivites since the Gibeonites were descended from the Hivites) tricked Joshua into making a treaty with them so that they wouldn't be slaughtered like all the other people who lived in Canaan. Saul, begrudg-ing this treaty, broke it and persecuted them because of it. If Rizpah had not acted, it is most likely that Saul's other descendants would have found revenge on the Gibeonites in return for the death of these seven sons, and the cycle would have continued.

But the cycle did not continue, because David buried not only Saul's descendants but also the bodies of Saul and Jonathan. In order to understand the significance of this we need to appreciate the importance of burial in this context. Burial was essential as a means of honour-ing the dead. Not only was it important to be buried but it was important to be buried with your family, hence all the references in the Books of 1 and 2 Kings to the Kings being buried with their ancestors. When David heard of Rizpah's actions he gathered together the bones of Saul's whole family (including Saul and his beloved Jonathan) and buried them together. What is intriguing is that he had not buried Jonathan before. It seems that the hatred of war and the victory had blinded him to the need to honour his dead friend. Rizpah's actions made David think again and act differently.

In the face of the grief and pain that Rizpah felt in the aftermath of Saul's death there was very little that she could do. What she did was all that she could do, and in doing it she stopped a blood feud in its tracks and per-suaded a King to change his ways. So whenever the words 'there's nothing *I* can do' come to mind, I remind myself of Rizpah and the unforeseen consequences that might just arise simply from doing the only thing I can do.

4 Insane generosity

John 6.5–11 When he looked up and saw a large crowd coming toward him, Jesus said to Philip, 'Where are we to buy bread for these people to eat?' He said this to test him, for he himself knew what he was going to do. Philip answered him, 'Six months' wages would not buy enough bread for each of them to get a little.' One of his disciples, Andrew, Simon Peter's brother, said to him, 'There is a boy here who has five barley loaves and two fish. But what are they among so many people?' Jesus said, 'Make the people sit down.' Now there was a great deal of grass in the place; so they sat down, about five thousand in all. Then Jesus took the loaves, and when he had given thanks, he distributed them to those who were seated; so also the fish, as much as they wanted.

For further reading: John 6.1–15

While we are on the subject of doing what you can, the other person who comes to mind is the young boy in John's account of the feeding of the five thousand. Unlike in the other three gospels, John attributes the bringing of the five loaves and two fishes to a single person: a young boy. Matthew, Mark and Luke, in contrast, imply that the food is the sum total of all the food available: all that brought by the disciples and people combined. Whether the giving of the loaves and fishes was down to the generosity of one boy or of more than one, the extraordinary nature of the generosity remains.

Anxiety about lack of food is one of those primal instincts that can easily rise to the surface. Even in our affluent society where studies estimate that we throw away 18 per cent of all food purchased, it doesn't take much for a stampede on the supermarkets. A fuel crisis or the threat of a few days of snow can see the shelves emptied almost instantaneously. Even at meals where the food is laid out buffet-style it is intriguing to see people sidling up and positioning themselves to ensure that they don't miss out on the nicest of the food available. If we're honest, we've probably all done it ourselves at one point or another, I know I have: casually strolling into position, while attempting to look nonchalant, to ensure that we get our own particular favourite food, which we fear someone else might consume before we do.

In the context of this, it becomes clear that a miracle happened even before Jesus' miracle of feeding – a miracle of generosity. John focuses this miracle down onto a single individual and as a result focuses our attention more fully onto this small miracle. You see, the natural and entirely understandable reaction in the face of the circumstances would have been for the boy to keep the food and eat it himself; or at most – given that five loaves and two fishes would have been too much for one person – to share it with those around him. It would have been natural because the boy would have known that his loaves and fishes could not have fed all that number of people. There was nothing that he could do for five thousand people, so wouldn't he be being more prudent if he kept it for his own small group?

Perhaps he didn't realize that no one else had brought food. Perhaps he assumed that his contribution was being matched around the other groups and that when all the contributions were gathered together there would have been much more. We will never know, but what we do know is that it was his act of insane, selfless generosity that allowed the rest to be fed. So often we are encouraged to be 'sensible' with our generosity, to offer things only if we are confident they can make a difference. What this story reminds us is that generosity in the economy of God is not about being sensible. God's generosity is insane and selfless – just like this young boy's – and summons us to respond like for like.

This story reminds us that we should never hold back from offering our small gift, even when we are confident that it will be insufficient for what is needed. The reason for this is because we can never know what God's miraculous, generous intervention can do with the smallest of things that we offer. What may be in our eyes so ridiculously small that it is barely worth mentioning, can in God's eyes be just the start that is needed to allow him to do the rest. We each have so much to offer in terms of time, talent, money, creativity, imagination, hope, and encouragement. No gift that we have to offer is ever too small for God. The young boy could never have guessed what his small gift could do, neither can we ... and that is precisely why we should give it anyway.

❧

5 And yet more generosity

Luke 8.1–3 Soon afterwards he went on through cities and villages, proclaiming and bringing the good news of the kingdom of God. The twelve were with him, as well as some women who had been cured of evil spirits and infirmities: Mary, called Magdalene, from whom seven demons had gone out, and Joanna, the wife of Herod's steward Chuza, and Susanna, and many others, who provided for them out of their resources.

Romans 16.1–2 I commend to you our sister Phoebe, a deacon of the church at Cenchreae, so that you may welcome her in the Lord as is fitting for the saints, and help her in whatever she may require from you, for she has been a benefactor of many and of myself as well.

I cannot be alone in the conversations I have with my children about money. The younger they are the more convinced they are that money, while not growing on trees, is endlessly made by the bank for our convenience. Once I said to one of my daughters that we couldn't have something because we didn't have the money. To which she, very pragmatically, responded that's OK we can go to that machine in the wall and they'll make us some more!

Although as we get older we become more realistic about money and its value, I'm not sure that we celebrate enough the generosity of those whose financial contributions allow so much to happen. In the previous section we noted the importance of the young boy in John's Gospel whose generosity with bread and fish allowed five thousand people to be fed. This section is also about generosity but this time about financial contributions not just contributions of food.

Much has been said about Mary Magdalene over the years, most of it based on the flimsiest of evidence. Mary has for centuries been thought to have been a 'fallen woman' or 'prostitute'. The evidence for this is, as I said above, at best flimsy and at worst preposterous. The connection seems to have been made through Luke 8. John's Gospel has an account of Mary (though this Mary is the sister of Martha and Lazarus not Mary Magdalene) anointing Jesus' feet and wiping it with her hair (John 11. 2 and 12.1–17). Luke 7.37–50 has a similar story, though this time the woman is unnamed and called simply 'a woman in the city who was a sinner'.

Luke 8.1-3 immediately follows this passage and names, among other women, Mary Magdalene. So with a leap worthy of an Olympic medal, Christian tradition has put together a Mary who anointed Jesus feet with a woman who was some kind of sinner, and arrived at Mary Magdalene as a prostitute. So Mary Magdalene has for hundreds and hundreds of years been depicted in various stages of undress and looking morally questionable.

In reality we know three things about Mary, none of which warrants such a description. We know that Jesus cured her of seven demons, we know that she was one of the faithful women who stayed by the cross as Jesus died and later went to his tomb and that she probably had sufficient resources to support Jesus and his disciples in his ministry.[2] It is this last quality that intrigues me. We often don't ask the question of how Jesus and his disciples survived their itinerant lifestyles. Luke suggests here that they did so with support, and that it was people like Mary, Joanna and other unnamed women who sacrificially supported them. You may be interested to know, in the light of the passage about Martha, which we explored in the previous chapter, that the verb used to describe what the women did here (*diakoneō*) is connected to the noun used to describe what Martha was distracted by (*diakonia*). As a result, just as a translation of what Martha may have been distracted by could be that she was distracted by 'much ministry', Mary and the other women may be said to have 'ministered' to Jesus out of their own resources. This is no small contribution and is a ministry worthy of

2 The question here is how far the description at the end of this verse 'who provided for them out of their resources' stretches backward. While it is possible that it just refers to the 'many others', the mention of Joanna the wife of Herod's steward suggests that she too is wealthy. If she is to be included in the description it is most likely that Mary is too.

deep respect – though all Mary Magdalene got was her reputation besmeared and dragged through the mud.

These were not the only women involved in the financial support of the work of the kingdom. Another hugely significance example of this is Phoebe, who is referred to in Romans 16.1-2. Much has been made of the reference here to Phoebe being a deacon (that word again – this time Phoebe is called a *diakonos* but the words are all connected), though precisely what this means in this period is hard to discern. In my view, however, not enough has been made of Phoebe being a *prostatis* as she is called at the end of 16.2. For a long, long time all the major English translations rendered this simply as 'helper' but the modern translations now, correctly, recognize that this is insufficient. The word has much more resonance than this and the English Standard Version is probably correct in translating it as 'Patron'. In the Roman world a Patron was a hugely significant figure who not only supported a wide range of artisans (from potters to poets) financially but also defended them politically should the need arise. In Romans 16.2 Paul commends Phoebe as a *prostatis* not only of himself but of others. In other words Phoebe supported a wide range of people connected to the church in Cenchreae (a port of Corinth) both financially and politically.

These passages are important for two reasons. The first, of course, is that they remind us to give thanks for all those who support the kingdom by giving financially to it and to recognize the deep importance of this kind of ministry. The second is that we see in them the vital role played by some key women in the early development of the Christian community and, in my view, we can't celebrate that enough.

❦

6 Companionship in the Gospel

2 Corinthians 2.12–13 When I came to Troas to pro-claim the good news of Christ, a door was opened for me in the Lord; but my mind could not rest because I did not find my brother Titus there. So I said farewell to them and went on to Macedonia.

What is your mental image of Paul? One of the most entertaining descriptions of him comes from the Acts of Paul and Thecla, which is a text written sometime in the second century AD. It is difficult to know how reliable it is, but it is relatively early and may have some foundation in history. The Acts of Paul and Thecla describe Paul as of middling height, with scanty hair, bowed legs, large eyes, eyebrows that meet in the middle and a long nose. If this description has any basis in fact, Paul was not the most physically attractive person in the world! It must be said that many people I talk to also do not attribute much personal charm to Paul either. Many people see him as arrogant, quite prickly, self-sufficient, not some-one whom it would be easy to befriend and certainly not someone who particularly needed company.

The more I've read of Paul, the more convinced I have become that this is the wrong perception of him. Paul is described in Acts regularly travelling with companions. Possibly even more important is the fact that most of Paul's epistles attribute the letters to Paul and someone else: 2 Corinthians, Philippians and Colossians refer to Timothy as well as Paul, 1 Corinthians has Sosthenes alongside Paul, Galatians 'all the members of God's fam-ily who are with me' and 1 and 2 Thessalonians make reference to Timothy and Silvanus. In Galatians 6.11 Paul even draws attention to the large letters with which he writes and most people assume that this means he did not physically write the rest of the letter but only picked up the pen for its final farewell. All of this gives the impression that Paul wrote his letters at the least in the company of others and most likely with some level of extra input into the writing.

None of this gives the impression of Paul as a lone wolf doing what he did without the companionship and support of others. For me one of the most moving references to Paul's need for support in ministry is the reference in 2 Corinthians 2.12–13. In this part of 2 Corinthians Paul begins to probe the breakdown of the relationship that has taken place between himself and the Corinthian community and to remind them that whatever their lack of trust for Paul, himself, the gospel that he preached remains reliable. In this part of the epistle we see more clearly than elsewhere into Paul's heart and into what hurts him the most.

It is very easy to assume that people whom we deem to be 'successful' (whatever we mean by that) are somehow more robust than we are ourselves; that people in positions of power and authority can take much more criticism than others can. The opening chapters of 2 Corinthians remind us that this is not the case. Even people like Paul got hurt by the breakdown of relationships and unjust allegations. In 2 Corinthians 2.12–13 he makes the most startling of admissions. He went to Troas to preach the gospel and found many opportunities to do this, but he couldn't do it because he couldn't find Titus there so he travelled onwards to Macedonia. What this seems to mean is that Paul – the greatest evangelist of all time – passed up the opportunity to preach the gospel because his friend Titus wasn't there.

Of course we don't know precisely why Paul couldn't preach without Titus. It might have been simply lack of companionship or it might have been that he was waiting for Titus to return from Corinth with a message about how his embassy to the Corinthians had gone. Either way, however, Paul allowed personal relationships to get in the way of his proclamation of the gospel. What Titus, Sosthenes, Timothy, Barnabas and countless others provided to Paul was the friendship and support that enabled him to continue his ministry. It is very striking that both in 1 Corinthians 12 and in Romans 12 where Paul lays out the gifts of the spirit, among what you might call the more glamorous gifts, are assistance or helping (1 Corinthians 12.28) and exhortation or encouragement (Romans 12.8). Paul himself knew how important these were because he needed them himself.

Although we may not put too much store by the simple ministry of being there for someone, encouraging them and helping them out when they need it, this is vital not only for the welfare of the church but for those engaged in challenging ministries of all kinds. People like Titus kept Paul's ministry going through the tough times and the good. I don't for a moment imagine it was easy. I am a huge fan of Paul and of his theology but recognize that he almost certainly wasn't easy to be around. As a result we need to give our thanks and respect to Titus, Paul's other companions and indeed to all those other unnamed and uncelebrated companions in the gospel who have encouraged, supported and enabled the preaching of the gospel down the centuries and to those who continue to do this today.

❦

We are notoriously bad at celebrating unsung heroes. Of course we are, if we weren't they wouldn't be 'unsung', but there is great virtue in taking time to appreciate the unsung heroes of our lives of faith, whether in the Bible or in our lives today. We need to become better at thanking and honouring those who get little if any notice, whose patient quiet service keeps the show on the road, who are as far from celebrities as you can get but who, nevertheless, are vital to God's mission in the world.

We do need to be better at celebrating such people but at the same time we also need to recognize that part of the essence of the kingdom of God is to be 'unsung'. The problem with our celebrity culture, which is as vibrant within the church as outside of it, is that it so often forgets that our calling as Christians is to be servants of all. This does not mean that we are called to be well-known, well-respected, often-thanked servants of all, but that we take on the role of a servant in all its aspects. One of these aspects is to go unnoticed. The best servants are those whose presence is barely discernible as they go about their business; the worst are those who advertise not only their presence but the trouble you are putting them to by sighing deeply and dragging their feet.

Part of the point of God's calling to each one of us is that we are called to be God's unsung heroes and we will know we are succeeding, not when people begin to notice us but when they begin to notice God.

PART TWO

Ordinary God

3

AN EVERYDAY GOD

In some ways it seems wrong to have a chapter, let alone a section or book entitled 'Ordinary' or 'Everyday' God. God is so clearly extraordinary in every way possible that it can't be right even to suggest that God might be in some way ordinary. Surely God is majestic, awe-inspiring and wonderful, not ordinary or every day? What strikes me from a reading of both the Old and the New Testaments is that, while it is absolutely right and proper that we experience awe and wonder when we contemplate who God is and what he has done, at the same time we need to take care that we do not box God into a gilded house in which he has no desire to be.

As human beings we have a natural instinct to organize and categorize; it helps us to understand the world and to feel as though it has some kind of order. The problem is that when we do this we tend to prescribe who people are and what we think they should do. We pigeonhole them and say 'if you are like this, then you cannot be like that'. Sometimes when we pigeonhole God we place him in majestic surroundings; we build him a place to dwell, where through beauty in art, music and liturgy, we can begin to offer back in worship our wonder at who he is and what he has done. This is absolutely appropriate until we move from there to an assumption that God *only* likes gilded buildings, fine art and exquisite music.

It seems to me that one of the lessons we struggle to comprehend is that God finds beauty in ordinary people doing his will ordinarily, in the things of earth being lived out to heavenly standards, and in justice and righteousness. There is nothing wrong at all in worshipping God in and through beauty, but we need to recognize that God's desire is to be worshipped in the beauty of holiness – a beauty that can just as easily be found in mud as in gold, in the everyday as in the special places we create for it. God it seems has never had the desire to be contained in the special places we create for him. Over and over again throughout the Bible we find examples of times when he felt the need to break out of the places into which humanity sought to lock him. Just as Jesus also had to escape people's desire to make him king and tie him down to an earthly throne with earthly expectations of all that what would entail. The biblical tradition bears witness to the ways in which God constantly resists being tied down in splendour and riches: being found as much, if not more so, in slums as royal palaces, in poverty as in wealth, in dishonour as honour, in humility and brokenness as much as in glory and nobility. The God we worship is extraordinary in every way and as an expression of this chooses to be found in our midst, an everyday God.

❧

1 The Sound of a Slight Whisper

1 Kings 19.9–12 At that place he came to a cave, and spent the night there. Then the word of the LORD came to him, saying, 'What are you doing here, Elijah?' He answered, 'I have been very zealous for the LORD, the God of hosts; for the Israelites have forsaken your cov-

enant, thrown down your altars, and killed your proph-
ets with the sword. I alone am left, and they are seeking
my life, to take it away.' He said, 'Go out and stand on
the mountain before the LORD, *for the* LORD *is about*
to pass by.' Now there was a great wind, so strong that
it was splitting mountains and breaking rocks in pieces
before the LORD, *but the* LORD *was not in the wind;*
and after the wind an earthquake, but the LORD *was*
not in the earthquake; and after the earthquake a fire,
but the LORD *was not in the fire; and after the fire a*
sound of sheer silence.

For further reading: 1 Kings 19.1–21

I was once in a cathedral for celebratory service. At the
end, as usual, the organ began to play. That day the
organist was clearly having fun and the voluntary was so
loud that my ribs shook. Behind me was a mother with a
small child. The child put his hands over his ears, looked
outraged and shouted over the organ music: 'Does God
have to be so noisy?' It struck me at the time as a great
question and one to which this particular passage has an
answer.

So often as human beings we need signs of grandeur
and awe to remind us that something is grand and awe-
inspiring. In the Old Testament, God's presence was associated with loud, dramatic weather. The sign of God's
presence was heralded by earthquakes, thunder and lightning. It is such a strong tradition that nearly all of the
major accounts which describe God's presence on earth
are accompanied by such things. Moses, receiving the law
on Mount Sinai, would hear God speaking in thunder
(Exodus 19.19); Ezekiel when he saw God seated on the
throne saw among many other things fire and lightning

(Ezekiel 1.13–14) and Job when he eventually encountered God heard him speak out of the whirlwind (Job 40.6). All this weather served to demonstrate the awe-inspiring nature of God's presence.

One of the reasons why this passage is so significant is that it serves as a reminder that God's presence can be accompanied by loud noise and grandeur but it doesn't have to be. God's presence can be accompanied by claps of thunder, or bolts of lightning but he doesn't need them. In answer to the little boy's question: no, God does not need to be noisy; sometimes it is us that needs God to be noisy to assure us of his magnificence but it is not something that God needs. Unlike the Gods of Canaan or other ancient religions, God is not tied to natural phenomenon. He is not like Ba`al, the Canaanite God, who was specifically associated with thunder. Part of what this passage was demonstrating was that God was as unlike Ba`al as it is possible to be. In this instance, unlike Ba`al, he was not tied to wind, earthquakes or fire.

As well as this, however, this passage is also communicating something else. Elijah is exhausted, physically and emotionally, by his battle with Jezebel and the prophets of Ba`al on the top of Mount Carmel (1 Kings 18.1–46) and, if truth be told, is feeling sorry for himself. Twice, before and after God's appearance, God asked Elijah: 'What are you doing here? (19.9 and 13), and Elijah gave the response that he has had a great battle with the prophets of Ba`al and now they (that is, Jezebel's people) are trying to kill him. In other words, he is hiding.

One of the intriguing features of this passage is that God's question has two possible meanings. It can mean, as the NRSV has it here, what are you doing here, or it can mean 'What is there for you here?' (literally the Hebrew means 'what to you here, Elijah?'). Elijah, it seems is so sunk in his misery and exhaustion that he cannot hear or perceive either God's underlying question, or indeed the answer to it, because the answer to 'what is there for you here, Elijah?' is the presence of the all-powerful and all-loving God. It is striking that God asks Elijah this question 'what is there for you here?' the first time – then shows him the answer by appearing – and then asks again. Elijah it seems has learnt nothing ... or at least not yet, since he gives the same answer as before. Though it is noticeable that God after his appearance to Elijah gives him his next impossible job (the crowning of new kings and the anointing of a successor) and he has the strength to continue onwards. All that has changed is Elijah's encounter with God which he experienced through ... what?

It is often the case, particularly in the Hebrew Old Testament but also in the Greek New Testament that the most important verses are the hardest to translate. This is especially true here. The King James Version translation is 'a still small voice' and was made especially beloved by the Wesley hymn 'Dear Lord and Father of Mankind', which talks of the 'still small voice of calm'. This is now thought not to be the best translation of the verse, since the word rendered 'voice' is actually better translated as 'sound'. The relevant words are 'sound', 'whisper' or 'silence' and 'fine', 'thin' or 'small'. So they mean something like the sound of a tiny whisper, or the sound of fine silence (the NRSV opted for sheer silence and the NIV a gentle whisper). If it's any comfort the Greek translation of the Old Testament seems to have struggled too and comes up with the 'sound of a small breeze'.

Hard though it may be to translate, the basic point is clear. What Elijah needed in his misery and exhaustion was not awe-inspiring thunder, or wonder-evoking lightning but the finest, gentlest, whispery, silence of God. Does God need to be noisy? Most definitely not – what

God did was communicate his presence in exactly the way that Elijah needed. Not in a great fanfare but in the most ordinary, yet profound, silence.

ᴄᵕᵎᵎᵕᴐ

2 I hate, I despise your festivals

Amos 5.21–24 I hate, I despise your festivals, and I take no delight in your solemn assemblies. Even though you offer me your burnt offerings and grain offerings, I will not accept them; and the offerings of well-being of your fatted animals I will not look upon. Take away from me the noise of your songs; I will not listen to the melody of your harps. But let justice roll down like waters, and righteousness like an ever-flowing stream.

For further reading: Amos 5.18–27

One of the constant challenges of translating into the modern idiom is the way in which language shifts and changes. This has never been more the case than now. As a result adaptations that were intended to sound more relevant, end up sounding out of place and discordant. The NRSV translation, 'I hate, I despise your festivals' updated as it was from 'feasts' to sound more contemporary now sounds, to me at least, as though God has got something against music festivals: God hates Glastonbury and Reading, and come to think of it he's not too keen on Greenbelt or Spring Harvest either. Of course, that isn't what Amos is saying here ... or is it?

The problem we can have when we hear the prophetic condemnations of the Old Testament is that we no longer think that feasts (or festivals) like Pentecost or Tabernacles, or burnt and grain offerings are the way to worship God. So of course he wouldn't like them would he? As most commentators on this passage observe, Amos' condemnation was deeply shocking and unnerving to his audience. The point is that the feasts and offerings were no more or less than what God had commanded them to do in the Torah. There was nothing wrong with them *per se* (even if there were hints of corruption floating around). What Amos was condemning was that the people of God had forgotten that God was not restricted to one place. They had reduced worship of God to the few times a year that they took their animals to be sacrificed, and overlooked the fact that the Torah has two equally important strands: worship of God and love of neighbour.

One of the features of the prophecies that come from the time of Amos (known collectively as the eighth-century prophets and including Amos, Hosea, Micah and Isaiah) are their vehement condemnations of the oppression, abuse and corruption that seem to have been widespread in this era. The people of God seem to have fallen into the trap of believing that worshipping God was all they needed to do. Amos' message here is that worshipping God without caring for your neighbour is abhorrent to God. Worship without justice, adoration without compassion are not only worthless, they are repugnant. God does not want to be worshipped by people whose lives do not reflect the principles of justice, righteousness and compassion.

The message that Amos is laying out here is that God insists that what we do on Monday is as important as what we do on Sunday, Saturday (or in this instance a feast day). God is as interested in the times when we are not worshiping formally as in the times when we are. In fact if the everyday lives that we live are not shot through with principles of justice and righteousness, then God will reject our worship outright. I remain convinced that

Amos' condemnation here is as relevant today as it ever was, and that God could just as easily say today: 'I hate, I despise your Christian festivals, I take no delight in your worship services and Eucharists. Even though you pray and offer beautiful worship, I will not accept it. Take away from me the noise of your songs (no need for changing these words!), I will not listen to the music of your organs and worship bands. But let justice roll down like waters, and righteousness like an ever-flowing stream.'

Our worship may have changed but the underlying issue has not. The people of God have always found it easier to obsess about the minutiae of 'perfect worship' than we have to pour over what acting justly really means; we have always found it easier to argue the benefits of hymns over songs; organ over worship band; liturgy over spirit-led worship – but run the risk of discovering that God has rejected the lot on the grounds of inadequate righteousness (which we should note is righteousness and not self-righteousness!).

Of course the question that always emerges for me when reflecting on this is how will I know? How will I know that my justice is rolling like waters and not dripping like a tap? How will I know if my righteousness is like an ever-flowing stream and not a dried-up ditch? It is all too easy to become obsessed with impossible levels of detail which actually detract from the whole point of the issue. Living a life of justice is not mechanistic: it is not to be found in how many bags of fairly traded coffee, tea and sugar you buy (though this isn't a bad start!). Living a life of justice and righteousness requires a transformation of attitude which removes my needs and desires from the centre of my life and replaces them with the needs of others. Living a life of justice and righteousness involves genuinely seeking the welfare of others – and in our modern global world this involves those who live thousands of miles away as well as those who live next door. God does not weigh our acts of justice like grains of rice which may or may not tip the scales into acceptability; instead he looks for lives shaped by the principles of justice and asks whether we spend as much time and attention ensuring that our justice is right as we do our worship. Our God, the everyday God, calls us to be everyday Christians and not just Sunday-best ones.

❧

3 A God who weaves

Psalm 139.13–16 For it was you who formed my inward parts; you knit me together in my mother's womb. I praise you, for I am fearfully and wonderfully made. Wonderful are your works; that I know very well. My frame was not hidden from you, when I was being made in secret, intricately woven in the depths of the earth. Your eyes beheld my unformed substance. In your book were written all the days that were formed for me, when none of them as yet existed.

Job 10.8–12 Your hands fashioned and made me; and now you turn and destroy me. Remember that you fashioned me like clay; and will you turn me to dust again? Did you not pour me out like milk and curdle me like cheese? You clothed me with skin and flesh, and knit me together with bones and sinews. You have granted me life and steadfast love, and your care has preserved my spirit.

One of the glories of growing up with the Scriptures, and hearing them read and discussed from an early age, is that some passages become deeply embedded in your soul. These passages shape your imagination and outlook. Psalm 139 with its beautiful imagery of creation is one of those passages for me. Of course the problem with this is that it lives so powerfully in my imagination that it has taken on a life of its own. What comes to mind whenever I hear this passage is a God, seated comfortably on his throne, with two large knitting needles, steadily knitting humanity into life. I can even hear the click of the needles as God rhythmically knits human beings ready for their mothers' wombs. I know of course that my imaginative picture of this passage is completely wrong but this doesn't, alas, make it any fainter in my mind.

What is remarkable in this passage is that though my very homely picture of a God sitting on a comfy throne, knitting away is wrong … it isn't that wrong. The images used both in Psalm 139 and in Job 10 are very ordinary images. The word translated 'knit' by nearly all of the English translations was chosen presumably because of its double meaning: not only meaning the act of knitting with needles but also referring to what bones do when they mend. The Hebrew word has no such double meaning and would be more accurately translated as 'wove'.[3] The word has the particular resonance of weaving together from a range of different colours. It is a very homely word used to describe the ordinary activity of weaving. The Job passage adds to this homely image a range of others. Here God creates humanity by shaping mud (10.9, as indeed God creates Adam in Genesis 2.7) and by curdling milk to make cheese as well as by weaving. What both Psalm 139 and Job 10 are doing is reminding us that the most

---

3 It should be noted that there is a slight difficulty with the word as this word in Hebrew could be from one of two completely different roots: one meaning to cover the other to weave. Scholars agree, however, that weave must be the right translation here.

extraordinary acts of God are to him the things of every-day living.

The images are of course metaphors and on one level it is ludicrous to compare God's act of creation to weaving and making cheese but the point that the Psalmist and the author of Job are trying to make is that what is for us a mind blowing act of extraordinary power, is for God the stuff of everyday existence. For us the miracle of conception and the growth of a baby in the womb is so wonderful it is impossible to comprehend, for God it is like weaving a garment or making cheese. For us the sky is too vast even to be able to see it, for God its creation was simply like putting up a tent (Psalm 104.2). This is an important aspect of the celebration of all things ordinary. What is ordinary for one person, is extraordinary for another person. God's on-going acts of creation are, for us, miraculous but for God they are commonplace. Ordinary is a relative term, anything we do regularly becomes ordinary, though for someone else it might be something they have never done and always wanted to.

The other reason I love both Psalm 139 and Job 10 is that the metaphors used here to describe God's creation of the world refer to tasks that would normally be left to women. They are the menial, simple tasks of everyday existence, often unheralded and unsung. It is intriguing that in using metaphors of God's creation the Psalmist and author of Job felt comfortable using images associated with women's roles to describe what God did. The effect of this for me is to elevate these 'menial' tasks into some-thing altogether more significant and to give them a status that otherwise they would not have. Using such meta-phors of God's creation implies that those who weave, who knit and sew, who cook and bake are not engaged in lowly, unimportant, insignificant tasks but are joining with God in the very act of creation. The description of

God engaging in 'ordinary' activities, transforms those ordinary activities into something extraordinary.

႘

4 What do you mean he's not here?

Matthew 2.1–6 In the time of King Herod, after Jesus was born in Bethlehem of Judea, wise men from the East came to Jerusalem, asking, 'Where is the child who has been born king of the Jews? For we observed his star at its rising, and have come to pay him homage.' When King Herod heard this, he was frightened, and all Jerusalem with him; and calling together all the chief priests and scribes of the people, he inquired of them where the Messiah was to be born. They told him, 'In Bethlehem of Judea; for so it has been written by the prophet: "And you, Bethlehem, in the land of Judah, are by no means least among the rulers of Judah; for from you shall come a ruler who is to shepherd my people Israel."'

One of the very obvious examples of God's love of the ordinary is of course the incarnation: God made flesh and living in our midst. In fact so obvious is it, that I spent a certain amount of time wondering whether to leave it out on the grounds that it might just be a bit too obvious. To do so, however, would be to leave a huge gap in the case for God's love of the ordinary. Jesus' birth is the key point, the clinching argument, the crucial piece of the jigsaw in the argument that God is an everyday God. God's willingness to send his son to live as a human being shouts to the rooftops the simple fact that God does not love grandeur, splendour and might, but he does love us. God loves us so much that he was prepared to swap his majestic throne for a feeding trough; everlasting worship by the angels for the incomprehension of his disciples; glory and honour for ignominy and shame. Jesus' birth in a small southern Judaean town where there wasn't even enough room for his family to stay so that Jesus had to be laid in a feeding trough must surely be one of the strongest examples there are that God is to be found in the ordinary and everyday.

The vignette in Matthew's Gospel which illustrates this so vividly is the Magi's visit to Herod's court in search of Jesus. Their logic, it seems, was impeccable. They knew of the birth of a new King in Judaea and so went to the King's palace to find him. Only to discover to their surprise and Herod's consternation, that he was most definitely not there. It's a little like having a guest of honour at a grand celebration and searching for them high and low, only to discover them in the kitchens doing the washing up (which incidentally is precisely the kind of behaviour which we, as followers of Jesus, are encouraged to have!).

The placing of Jesus' kingship next to Herod's emphasizes the contrast between the two. Herod had no real right to be king. He was neither from the line of David nor a member of the Hasmonean dynasty.[4] But somehow he had managed to persuade the Romans to allow him to rule anyway. The sources from the period suggest a man who was terrified of losing what was not really his in the first place. He surrounded himself with riches and symbols of power, and killed anyone who appeared to threaten his power. Overcome by fear that he would lose what he loved so much he even killed his wife Marimane and sons when they became too popular.

---

4 The Hasmoneans were the descendants of the Maccabees who had ruled in Judaea before the invasion of the Romans.

In great contrast Jesus was born with nothing of his own – not even a cradle to sleep in – he declared himself to be the servant of all and laid down his life for those who sought to stand in his way. Paul's phrase in Philippians 2.6 seems to sum up the contrast best. Jesus, though in the form of God, did not consider equality with God anything to be clutched or held on to; Herod, probably because he had no right to his position at all, clutched hard at his position with everything that he had.

The birth, life, ministry and death of Jesus all point to a Jesus who was not only unafraid of the ordinary but who positively embraced it. At the start of his life the Magi looked for him in the wrong place, and I suspect we have been doing the same ever since. Jesus has never been found in grand palaces, surrounded by servants and wealth. From his birth onwards Jesus was to be found precisely in those places where you wouldn't naturally look for a King, with the poor and outcast, the marginalized and oppressed. Jesus' presence among the unloved and unvalued of his day serves as a constant reminder to us that Jesus has never been found where we might expect a king to be and if we want to find him then we have to be prepared to look for him elsewhere.

꧁꧂

5 Sliced white or ciabatta?

John 6.32–35 Then Jesus said to them, 'Very truly, I tell you, it was not Moses who gave you the bread from heaven, but it is my Father who gives you the true bread from heaven. For the bread of God is that which comes down from heaven and gives life to the world.' They said to him, 'Sir, give us this bread always.' Jesus said to them, 'I am the bread of life. Whoever comes to me will never be hungry, and whoever believes in me will never be thirsty.'

For further reading: John 6.1–58

John's Gospel is, we are often told, the 'spiritual gospel'. Many people think that it is the product of years of reflection and thought which over time became honed, and written down in the form that we now have. I don't for a moment doubt that this is true. There is something about the reflective quality of John's Gospel that makes you feel as though it contains theology that has been long savoured, prayed about and reflected upon. It is a mistake, however, to confuse 'spiritual' with 'ethereal' or 'lacking in substance'. It never ceases to intrigue and entertain me that the 'I am' sayings are so gritty and earthy.

If I were asked to imagine the kind of 'I am' sayings that would fit with the overall tone of John's Gospel they would be abstract and profound, like 'I am love'; 'I am the source of all being'; 'I am mercy and compassion'. Instead, although some 'I am' sayings are more abstract ('I am the resurrection and the life' John 11.25; 'I am the way, the truth and the life' John 14.6), some of them are about as ordinary as you can get. Jesus describes himself as light (John 8.12); a gate (John 10.7); a shepherd (John 10.11 and 14); a vine (John 15.1); and, of course, as bread. Elsewhere Jesus also describes what he gives to the world as a gushing spring of water (John 4.14). These are no grand, conceptual ideas communicating something ethereal about the essence of God made flesh, they are simple, clear and down to earth.

These days certain supermarkets stock a 'basics' or 'essentials' range which contains those everyday ingredients that everyone needs, for less money than usual.

I am always entertained to see what supermarkets consider to be basic or vital for everyday living: apparently chocolate mousse, mozzarella pearls and croissant are all basic requirements for living. Jesus' essentials seem to me to be far more essential than that. Light, nourishment, refreshment and protection are among the things that Jesus, the great 'I am', provide for us. Jesus doesn't offer us the extras that make life more fun but which we don't really need. The Jesus of John's Gospel offers us the most ordinary things possible for our well-being and survival: the ability to see where we are going; inner nourishment; never ending refreshment; and a shepherd who not only cares for his sheep but protects them from those who would break in and cause them harm.[5]

One of the things I love about John 6 is that what Jesus offers might be just what we need for everyday existence but it is far from basic. Earlier in John 6 (verses 1–16) is the account of the feeding of the five thousand. There John tells us about Jesus' provision of enough food for five thousand from five loaves and two fish. Following that, the people are so excited by Jesus that they pursue him, and when they find him the conversation about Jesus being the bread of life takes place. As this is John's Gospel there are many ironic misunderstandings, John makes it clear that the people think that Jesus is offering them a permanent miracle of long-life bread, which in a way he is but the point is this is inner not outer nourishment; food for the soul not the body which as the gospel makes clear is far more important.

---

5 One of the intriguing features of John 10.1–17 is that Jesus describes himself both as the Good Shepherd and as the gate. The best explanation for this is that in the wilderness, shepherds would have had to extemporize in order to make a sheepfold for the night, gathering thorn bushes etc. to form the walls of the sheep-pen. The entrance would have been quite vulnerable, though, and the shepherd who really cared about the sheep might have lain down in the doorway (becoming the gate) to protect them.

What also goes on is that the Greek word for bread changes. The bread that the young boy brought at the feeding of the five thousand was barley loaves: the most basic bread available (John 6.9). It often contained grit and other additional matter which ground down the teeth and sat very heavily in the stomach. What the people who pursued Jesus were after was more utterly basic barley bread; what Jesus offered them as the bread of life (John 6.35) was top-quality bread made from wheat, not barley, and soft not hard and indigestible. It is hard to think of a modern equivalent, since all our bread these days is of reasonable quality, but the contrast is between something which is filling but not very nourishing and something top of the range, which is both filling and nourishing. The nourishment that Jesus gives us may be essential but it is not basic – it is the best quality available.

The Jesus of John's Gospel makes clear that God made flesh, the Word in our midst, might be beyond our imagining but he is no other-worldly being, a God striding over the face of the earth,[6] he is fully and truly human and, as a human being understands deeply our human needs and concerns. Not only does he do that but he provides us with everything we need for our existence. Jesus the great 'I am' offers the best range of essentials possible.

❧

6 Mud pies

John 9.6–7 When he had said this, he spat on the ground and made mud with the saliva and spread the mud on the man's eyes, saying to him, 'Go, wash in the

6 As he was famously described by the German theologian Ernst Käsemann in his book *The Testament of Jesus*, SCM Press, 1968.

pool of Siloam' (which means Sent). Then he went and washed and came back able to see.

For further reading: John 9.1–41

Not long ago I met up again with some of the people from the ante-natal class I attended when my oldest daughter was born. Eleven years on we reflected a little about what we *said* we would never do as parents and then confessed whether in fact we did do those things or not. One thing in particular stood out ... we had all sworn before our children were born that we would never, ever, under any circumstances lick a tissue and wipe some dirt off our children's faces. We all remembered this from our own childhoods and swore we would not inflict it upon our own children. Some were able to say, with pride, that they had kept that promise, others of us had to admit – more shamefacedly – that we had not.

None of us, however, had to admit that we had used spit to put dirt onto our children's faces as Jesus does here to the man born blind in John 9. Every time I read or hear this passage I wonder what the blind man thought about this method of his healing. Simply the thought of being healed with mud encrusted spit makes my toes curl. Could Jesus not have chosen another method? Did it have to be so earthy, so dirty and did it have to involve saliva? The answer of course is yes it did. Back again in John's Gospel we encounter a Jesus who not only used down-to-earth, gritty analogies for who he was, but who used gritty, down-to-earth methods to heal people too. While Jesus could have healed the man from afar (as he demonstrates in, for example, the healing of the Centurion's servant in Matthew 8.1–13), many of his healings involve touch. In fact it is this touch that is often so vital in Jesus' healings.

It is easy for us to become too hung up, too focused on the miraculous nature of the healing. This is hardly surprising given the decades of scepticism that have surrounded Jesus' miracles. In a context in which the miracles themselves have been questioned, and then questioned again, it is unsurprising that we have become over focused on whether they happened or not. The danger of this is that we then overlook other elements of the miracles which are just as important as the fact that they are miraculous. So often the hidden sub-narrative of the healing miracles is one of loneliness.

Loneliness has always been – and in fact continues to be – a major consequence of illness. Illness isolates and cuts people off from others both physically and emotionally. This was especially true during the time of Jesus when illness was seen as a cause of impurity, something that prevented you from worshipping in the temple. This is why many of the healing narratives in the gospel involve being declared clean by the priests in the temple. The people healed by Jesus became whole not just physically but emotionally as a result of their healing. They were offered the chance of re-integration into the society in which they lived. As a result it really mattered that Jesus touched them. Jesus' touch brought healing but it also signalled an end to loneliness and isolation. Could Jesus have healed people another way? Possibly, but if he had it might not have communicated as much to us about Jesus' desire to draw people back into the heart of their communities.

The healing of the man born blind in this story is centered around Jesus' touch. I suspect that my squeamishness about Jesus using mud and spit to do it says more about me than about either Jesus or the man. The point is that the man being healed probably didn't care how he was healed and Jesus would have known that. The man's need was far greater than his desire for things to happen nicely. There certainly seems to be a correlation in the gospels between people's need for Jesus' help and their ability to encounter him for who he was, rather than for who they thought he should be. One of the striking features of Mark's Gospel is that groups, like the Pharisees or the Scribes, the crowd and even the disciples were intrigued by Jesus but couldn't comprehend who he really was. The people who did comprehend him were those who, though being outsiders, needed him most (for example the Gerasene demoniac, Mark 5.1–20, or the Syrophoenician woman, Mark 7.24–30).

One of my favourite parts of Eugene Petersen's translation of the Bible, *The Message*, is his translation of Matthew 5.3, 'Blessed are the poor in spirit', which he renders, 'Blessed are those who know their need of God.' This seems to resonate with this theme here. Sometimes our problem is that we don't need God quite enough, or at least not enough to allow God to be the everyday God that he is. We ask for God's help without the mud and the spit. We want the sanitized, hygienic help of God, not the gritty, down-to-earth help that he offers. Jesus, now as then, offers us inclusion, love and healing, but not in fancy packaging. The question that we face is how much we need it and whether we'll accept it mud, spit and all.

❦

The everyday God whom we worship doesn't, it seems, feel bound by niceties and protocol, and contrary to our best attempts seems effortlessly to avoid being constricted in gilded palaces or temples. God is truly an everyday God and challenges us to respond by being everyday people in both senses of the word.

The God who came to earth to live among us was not and is not afraid of the ordinary things of life. He does not need fine settings or loud noises. He came to earth not offering abstract ideas or fancy theology but the essentials we need to survive. He came yearning to draw us back into relationship with himself and with one another, and used every means possible to achieve this – even mud and spit. The everyday God whom we worship was not squeamish and calls us similarly not to steer clear of the ordinary things of life but to embrace them and through them to bring transformation to the world.

At the same time God is as concerned with what we do every day of our lives as he is with what we do when we set aside time specifically to worship him. Even more than this, he is so concerned with what we do on the ordinary days that he will reject our worship if it is not built on the firm foundation of justice and righteousness in every part of our lives.

Our everyday God calls us to be people who embrace the everyday, every day of our lives, and in doing so we become the extraordinary people that he longs for us to be.

4

AN ORDINARY KINGDOM

I regularly find myself entertained by what are to my mind, unnecessary warnings that appear on packing and containers. So, for example, on take-away coffee cups you might find the warning: 'Caution, contents may be hot'; or on a set of kitchen knives the advice that the blades may be sharp. On both of these I feel that I might have been able to work this out for myself. In a similar vein, however, whenever I say the Lord's Prayer I ponder about whether it should have a health warning stamped across it.

We are so familiar with the words that it is easy to miss the radical, world-changing nature of that for which we pray. Every time we say the Lord's Prayer we pray, apparently fervently, for the coming of God's kingdom on earth as it is in heaven, and I wonder how much we mean it. Are we absolutely sure that we want God's kingdom to come on earth? Of course, in principle we do but in practice are we prepared for the disruption, the life-changing consequences and the challenges that always accompany God's kingdom? Are we ready for the way in which God's kingdom will disrupt our lives, turning our comfortable certainties upside down? Are we ready for the kinds of people that God's kingdom will attract? The parables of the kingdom that we will explore in this next chapter suggest to me that before we pray the Lord's Prayer we should take a deep breath, proceed with caution and be absolutely sure that we really mean what we say.

One of the striking things about these parables is that, like many of Jesus' 'I am' sayings, they involve ordinary things like seeds, yeast and a net. It is hardly surprising that the kingdom of our everyday God is best described with such everyday things, but it is. God's kingdom, like God himself, is not reserved for the important and well-healed of our world but for the outcast, the marginal and oppressed and it is right therefore that it is compared to everyday things.

ᶜᵛᵒᵏᵛ

1 The Kingdom of Heaven is like a weed?

Matthew 13.31-32 He put before them another parable: 'The kingdom of heaven is like a mustard seed that someone took and sowed in his field; it is the smallest of all the seeds, but when it has grown it is the greatest of shrubs and becomes a tree, so that the birds of the air come and make nests in its branches.'

My husband and I have had an allotment for the past three years and, as a result, now feel that we know a lot more about weeds than we ever thought we would. Weeds are remarkable ... and we often express the wish that the plants we grow were as persistent and verdant as our weeds. One of the most striking features of weeds is their persistence, tiny pieces of root or the smallest seed can ensure their survival for the next year, and the next ...

The traditional view of the parable of the mustard seed is that God's kingdom is like a mustard plant because it grows from small beginnings to something tall and majestic which offers shelter in its branches. On this view, the mustard tree is a gentle pastoral image and focuses on growing from small beginnings into something large which can offer shelter. In recent years, however, a growing number of scholars have begun to suggest that the parable of the mustard seed is much more radical than people have traditionally believed.

In fact, various references to the mustard plant in ancient sources suggest that it might be much less welcome to those working the ground than the traditional view implies. The Roman writer Pliny the Elder wrote a natural history in which he described the mustard plant as growing wild. Once it was planted, he commented, it was impossible to get rid of because when its seeds fell they germinated at once. In other words, while not quite a weed it is one of those plants that you must plant with care because you will never get rid of it. An equivalent for us might be mint, which though useful will spread and take over any bed in which you plant it unless you are very careful.

This changes this parable quite significantly. It begins the same. The Kingdom of Heaven is like a tiny seed, which germinates quickly and grows to full size swiftly. Once this has happened, you will never get rid of it. Its seeds will fall constantly, so that plants spring up all over the place. On one level this is immensely reassuring. It can often feel as though the responsibility for bringing God's kingdom on earth is entirely down to us, and that one slip will mean that it will retreat once more to the heavenly realms. This interpretation of the parable reminds us that, while we are called to strive as far as we can to bring God's kingdom into the places where we live, it is no tender plant that needs just the right soil, exactly the right amount of water and sun or it will die. The kingdom is more akin to mint than dahlias, and dandelions than geraniums. Once established, it is exceedingly difficult to eradicate.

On another level, however, this parable is much more challenging and suggests that the kingdom is not always welcome. If the Kingdom of Heaven has qualities that are like a weed, then its attraction to birds may be something that you don't want. As any gardener will tell you, the last thing you want in the middle of your nicely ordered patch is something that gives shelter to birds, since then they have an easy perch from which they can swoop down and consume your seedlings and berries. The image here may be of a fast-growing plant that suddenly provides unexpected shelter for birds in the middle of your cornfield.

If this is true, the parable is saying that Kingdom of Heaven will attract to the shelter of its branches those whom you might not want in your nice, tidy patch; those who will disrupt your gardening, and those whom you might under other circumstances seek to drive away. If this is right, Jesus is reminding us here that the Kingdom of Heaven might, in reality, be something which we think we want (mustard after all has its uses in cooking) but turns out to be a bit of a nuisance.

As I pray the Lord's Prayer and ask for God's kingdom to come on earth, I often look out at my fellow nice tidy Christians, in our nice tidy churches and wonder whether we know what we're asking for. Are we really prepared for the disruption that the kingdom brings? If the kingdom attracts the kind of people with whom Jesus spent his days, the outcast and poor, the prostitutes and sinners, then might we just regret it if God does listen to our prayer for the coming of the kingdom and answer it? As I said in the introduction, the Lord's Prayer needs to be prayed with caution, because one day God just might listen to us.

❧❀❧

2 And it is like yeast

Matthew 13.33 He told them another parable: 'The kingdom of heaven is like yeast that a woman took and mixed in with three measures of flour until all of it was leavened.'

I remember as a child watching my mum getting yeast ready to make bread. She didn't use the fast acting stuff you can buy these days. Instead she would dissolve the yeast in a warm, sugar water solution and put it in a warm place for it to begin acting, and if she forgot it the whole lot would bubble over the top of the jug making a glorious yeasty mess. Yeast is intriguing and entrancing, given the right conditions, it lives and grows ... and smells heavenly.

It is rather interesting to have the parable of the mustard seed and the parable of the yeast (or leaven) right next to each other in Matthew's Gospel, since the parallels and contrasts are intriguing.[7] Like the mustard seed, yeast grows quickly and takes over; unlike mustard, yeast needs exactly the right conditions for it to do so. Like mustard, yeast was regarded as either good or bad depending on the circumstances; unlike mustard, it is a very domestic image. The similarity between these two parables suggests that they refer to similar features in God's kingdoms, which are that the kingdom grows secretly and quickly.

While this is true each parable has a slightly different emphasis. The mustard seed seems to me to be a challenging parable reminding us that the kingdom is as robust as a weed and not easily destroyed, but also that with it come unforeseen consequences (in the form of birds

---

7 It is probably worth noting that Mark doesn't have this parable and as a result scholars think it unlikely that Jesus said them together even though Matthew records them together here.

nesting in its branches). The parable about yeast seems to be more reassuring than this. Both elsewhere in the New Testament and in Rabbinic literature yeast is often used to refer to the contagion of evil. Take for example Matthew 16.6 (also repeated in Mark 8.15 and Luke 12.1), which warns the disciples to beware of the yeast of the Pharisees and Sadducees. The idea behind this is that hypocrisy, deceit and slander are toxic and contagious and can quickly spread to poison the whole.

As a result, the use of yeast here is startling. It is so often used as a by-word for evil that using it here for the kingdom should come as something of a shock (though it doesn't to us as we are now so used to thinking of it as an analogy to the kingdom that it doesn't seem even mildly surprising). The image has a subversive power. The kingdom, Jesus is saying, is as powerful, as contagious and spreads as quickly as hypocrisy, deceit and slander. There is no need to fear the contagion of hypocrisy, deceit and slander, since the kingdom acts as strongly as they do. It grows as silently but as effectively as evil does.

Equally importantly, you can't always see the action of yeast simply by sitting and watching it. A loaf that is rising doesn't look as though it is rising until you go away and come back an hour later when it will be double the size it was before. In other words, just because you cannot see the kingdom growing its subversive message of integrity in the face of hypocrisy, truth in the face of deceit, and encouragement in the face of slander, it does not mean that it is not growing. This is a parable which suggests that we need to trust the kingdom to be as powerful as the forces we fear, even if we cannot see it growing before our eyes.

This seems to me to be a vitally important message for our times. It is so easy to be disheartened by the regular news reports of the failure of Christianity in the twenty-first century, the decline in the number of worshippers and the wane of influence over a society that is no longer interested in 'the church'. While we need to remind ourselves, firmly and regularly, that the Church and the kingdom are not exactly the same – the kingdom can, of course, be found in the Church but it can also be found outside it – this image of the silent but effective growing of the kingdom is important. Wherever the kingdom is truly to be found, it will grow even if we cannot see its growth.

Another important aspect of the parable is the quantities involved. Three measures of flour is a ridiculous amount of bread to make. The great parable scholar Joachim Jeremias suggests that three measures of flour would feed a hundred people. The woman hiding the yeast in the flour was preparing for a feast not for breakfast. When Jesus first spoke the parable, those involved in proclaiming the kingdom were very few in number, and yet this parable suggests that this is no problem at all. The leaven of the kingdom hidden in the dough of the world, in which they lived, grew and grew from small beginnings to affect the whole. No matter how small the start, no matter how tentative the beginning, no matter whether we can see it or not, the kingdom *will* grow wherever it is embedded and it *will* affect the whole.

༒

3 It is also like someone else's treasure

Matthew 13.44 *'The kingdom of heaven is like treasure hidden in a field, which someone found and hid; then in his joy he goes and sells all that he has and buys that field.'*

Every now and then, when reading the Gospels we come across something really shocking; something that throws us off course and challenges the way in which we see the world. In my experience this happens more often in the gospel parables than in any other form of writing. In a way this is the point of parables. The Greek word from which we get our English word parable means thrown alongside and this, in my view, sums up what parables are about. Jesus throws alongside a range of different images, which we then have to struggle to make sense of in the light of what else we know about the kingdom. The problem we often face is that we are now so familiar with the gospel parables that we don't really struggle anymore. We sit and listen to the kingdom being described as a seed, yeast, a pearl, a net, etc ... while barely turning a hair. Indeed, one of the valuable things about the re-interpretation of the parable of the mustard seed that I talked about above is that it comes as a bit of a shock and forces us back to wrestle with how the kingdom might possibly be compared to a weed.

One of the parables which, for me, has never lost this troubling edge is the parable of the treasure hidden in a field. In a way it doesn't really fit in this chapter. This chapter is meant to be about ordinary parables of the kingdom, and someone finding treasure in a field does not seem to fit into this category. The event of finding something buried in a field is not ordinary nor is the treasure that is found ordinary either. Nevertheless, I want to include it here because it is such an important parable for helping us to recognize the struggle that we should engage in with all the parables. We need to take the shock factor back from this parable to all Jesus' other parables and to feel again, with Jesus' first hearers, the incredulity evoked by God's kingdom being compared to such ludicrous things.

The problem with the treasure in the field parable is that it treads right on the borders of morality: surely the man should have reported the treasure when he found it? Wasn't he committing fraud by not mentioning it? The whole image is unsettling and slightly disturbing. In a world before banks were widespread,[8] treasure was often hidden in the ground. Indeed, in the Copper Scroll found in the caves at Qumran, is a detailed description of where to find a hoard of gold and silver which had been hidden. Burying treasure in a field was the ancient equivalent of putting it under your mattress. It kept it safe, or as this parable illustrates safe-ish. The danger attached to it is that someone might come along and discover it. The logic of this particular parable must surely be that the treasure did not belong to the person who was selling the field but to someone else who, probably because they did not own a field of their own, buried their treasure there.

This parable also sheds interesting light on the parable of the talents[9] in Matthew 25.14–29 (and also in Luke 19.12–28). In that parable a landowner gave money to three servants. The one with the least money buried it in the ground. The danger of someone finding your money that you had hidden in the ground must have been widely known, so the servant with the one talent was not just being lazy but taking a great risk, since he risked his talent being found and taken as happened in this parable.

---

8 It is worth noting that in Luke's version of the parable of the talents, Luke 19.12–28, the landowner makes mention of the fact that the servant who buried his coins could have put his money into a bank, literally the Greek says 'table'. This refers to the tables of the money changers and lenders. It was against Jewish law to lend money to other Jews for interest but you could lend to non-Jews for interest. Thus the landowner is effectively saying, at the very least you could have lent it to Gentiles for a profit.

9 A talent was a Greek coin which was worth about 5,000 denarii; Matthew 20.2 refers to a denarius as a day's wage. Even one talent, then, was quite a lot of money.

All of this suggests that this parable is in fact more ordinary than we might at first imagine, since it refers to a situation that may not have been all that unknown.

The point of this parable is not the question of whether you should keep the discovery of a treasure trove in a field quiet before you buy the field but the level of attention that you give to that discovery. Jesus' parable here suggests that the discovery of the kingdom should cause the same level of excitement, focus and determination as the discovery of £100,000 might elicit. Imagine how you might react if you discovered £100,000 in the cellar of a house you went to view, especially if you realized that it would still be there if you bought the house. This is the kind of reaction that the kingdom should evoke in us, not least because it is a treasure far more valuable than any amount of money.

The question that resonates so strongly in this parable is how far would we go for the sake of the kingdom? How many rules might we break? How far beyond the limits of 'polite' society might we stray? What is the kingdom worth for us? Do we strive for it as much as we might for 5p or as much as for £100,000 or more? No matter how often I hear this parable, I feel deeply uncomfortable not only about the question it asks but about the answer I might give.

⁕

4 That is so unfair!

Matthew 20.10–16 "*Now when the first came, they thought they would receive more; but each of them also received the usual daily wage. And when they received it, they grumbled against the landowner, saying,*

*'These last worked only one hour, and you have made
them equal to us who have borne the burden of the day
and the scorching heat.' But he replied to one of them,
'Friend, I am doing you no wrong; did you not agree
with me for the usual daily wage? Take what belongs
to you and go; I choose to give to this last the same as I
give to you. Am I not allowed to do what I choose with
what belongs to me? Or are you envious because I am
generous?' So the last will be first, and the first will be
last."*

For further reading: **Matthew 20.1–16**

You won't be in a household with children for very long
before the cry 'But that's not fair' arises. Children have
a very strong sense of justice, at least as far as their own
rights are concerned. They watch with beady eyes to
ensure that another member of the family does not get
a bigger slice of cake than they do, a later bed-time than
they have, or something else similar. Children seem to
take great care to ensure that their own rights are respect-
ed and that justice is done. In reality, it is not just children
who do this but adults too. It is simply that we either
couch our cries of 'That's not fair' in more sophisticated
language or keep our complaints more to ourselves, or at
least to those who will agree with us.

It is an illustration of the power of the parable of the
labourers in the vineyard that every time this passage is
read in church, I end up having long conversations with
people about whether it is really fair or not. Somehow
this parable pushes people's buttons in a way the finding of buried treasure in a field does not. Perhaps this is
because few of us would bury our treasure in a field and
risk its discovery by someone else; whereas we all feel

the injustice of not getting comparable wages or benefits with our colleagues when we work. The fascinating thing about this parable is that it manages to tap straight back into that childhood sense of fairness and justice in a way that we feel emotionally, rather than just intellectually.

The parable seems to say that the Kingdom of Heaven is not fair, or at least it is not fair according to our principles of fairness and justice. Our principles of fairness involve ensuring that I get my 'rights', that you get no more than I do, and that, if the rules change, my own position increases accordingly. To use a more domestic image, this parable is a little like me having a cake for my birthday and inviting my friends to share it with me. Then, counting carefully how many people are present, slicing the cake evenly into the appropriate number of pieces, and sharing it out; but, when handing it round suddenly deciding to be generous and to give my piece, as well as their piece to one person around the table. In this case those who got the first pieces might feel short changed, in that I had given them what appeared to be 'fair' but then changed the rules.

The kingdom, Jesus says here, is not about strict numeric fairness but about God's generosity; a generosity which over and over again demonstrates itself to reach ridiculous levels. God never gives one where he could give ten; and never ten where he could give a hundred. God's kingdom is already a place in which overwhelming generosity is given and received. Stopping to count whether you have received a fraction more generosity than I have is missing the point entirely. Indeed the language of the Greek text is even more hard hitting than this.

In the NRSV the landowner asks the grumbling labourers: 'Are you envious because I am generous?' The Greek more literally says: 'Is your eye evil because I am good?' The word good (*agathos*) is deeply connected to generosity, unselfishness and productivity. Intriguingly the 'evil eye' is an idiom that implies the opposite of good. In the Old Testament and in Rabbinic literature the evil eye is connected to selfishness, covetousness and hatred of others. In other words, the grumbling labourers have turned the landowner's good into evil by their attitude.

The Kingdom of Heaven is marked by God's generosity. A generosity which is not fair but is overwhelmingly munificent; it is not even but it is vast. Stopping to count whether I've got as much as you, not only prevents me from receiving what God is offering but also turns it from something good, unselfish and productive into something self-centred, covetous and involving hatred. The whole point about the Kingdom of Heaven is that it is not fair. In it, God does not give us what we deserve. The kingdom has nothing to do with 'fairness' and everything to do with generosity.

ლრდ

5 On caring and celebrating!

Luke 15.1–13 Now all the tax collectors and sinners were coming near to listen to him. And the Pharisees and the scribes were grumbling and saying, 'This fellow welcomes sinners and eats with them.' So he told them this parable ...

For further reading: Luke 15.1–10

Jesus didn't actually tell them one parable but, according to Luke, three: those that we normally call the parables of the lost sheep, the lost coin and the prodigal son. In a way these parables are companion parables to the parable of the treasure in the field (and the pearl of great price which we haven't looked at), in that the Matthean parables talk about finding something you didn't have before and the Lukan ones about what you do after you lose something. The result in all of them is similar – when you have found what you seek, you throw caution to the wind and celebrate! Taken altogether these parables push us towards nurturing the right attitude of celebration so that we learn to celebrate the things of the kingdom properly. We learn to recognize the value of the kingdom and do everything we can to gain it and we learn to recognize the people of the kingdom and celebrate their presence. They seem to suggest that we should become communities in which celebration is an 'ordinary' activity, ordinary as in regular, expected and every day.

I sometimes wonder whether, as Christians, we look enough like people primed and ready for a celebration; or indeed whether we celebrate enough. These parables all point to the importance of celebrating the kingdom as and where we find it. Jesus found it with the tax collectors and sinners and so feasted with them. The shepherd celebrated when he found his sheep. The woman threw a party when she found her coin, as did the father of the son who returned. Over the years, these parables have come to be seen more as parables about finding than about celebrating but it seems to me that the connecting thread that runs through them all is one of celebration.

While it is easy to say that we must all celebrate more, in reality this is much harder than at first meets the eye. I've certainly been at gatherings which are purportedly for a celebration but at which no one feels like celebrating. Maybe the people for whom the party has been thrown have had an argument, or everyone is tired and not in the mood, but a celebration without a celebratory spirit is grim indeed.

This, obviously, is not what Jesus is talking about here. Part of the inner dynamic of all of these parables is that the celebration is genuine and heartfelt. There is a strong link between the care for what has been lost, the crazy lengths someone will go to find it, and the subsequent joy they experience. Take, for example, the parable of the lost sheep. We are so used to Jesus' question now: 'Which one of you, having a hundred sheep and losing one of them, does not leave the ninety-nine in the wilderness and go after the one that is lost until he finds it?' (Luke 15.4) that we all nod wisely and say yes of course we would. But the real answer is: 'Are you mad? No one in their right mind would leave ninety-nine sheep in the wilderness, while looking for one.' Jesus' original audience must have looked at Jesus with blank incomprehension. Of course they wouldn't, what on earth was he thinking?

But the craziness of the action alerts us to the genuineness of the celebration. Of course no one in their right mind would leave ninety-nine sheep in the wilderness while they went off to look for one; but someone out of their mind with worry might. In the same way the woman's evident concern for the loss of a drachma communicates how much she needed it. A drachma was about a day's wages. Its loss would have been inconsequential for a rich person but someone with very little money at all (just ten days' wages saved up) would have scoured the whole house looking for it.[10] Again the father's celebration for his son who had been lost and now was found came from deep within.

The challenge for those of us who seek to be communities of the kingdom is whether we care enough to

---

10 It is highly unlikely that the popular and romantic interpretation which has the ten coins as part of a wedding headdress is correct. This is a practice among modern Bedouin women not Jewish women of the first century.

celebrate. Do we care enough, like the shepherd of the parable, to throw caution to the wind and engage in some hare-brained scheme for the sake of the kingdom? Do we care enough to be so joyful, like the woman who probably blew her hard-earned cash in celebrating with her neighbours, that we cannot help our celebration when we find those who are lost? Do we care enough that we risk alienating those, like the elder son, who have never gone away, in our joy that someone who was lost has been found?

The scribes and the Pharisees didn't care at all and so could not begin to understand Jesus' feasting with the tax collectors and sinners. Celebration, Jesus suggests here, is directly connected to how much we care. This makes the question of whether we are communities of celebration an even more pointed question than it already was.

❧

6 On losing and finding

Luke 15.6 And when he comes home, he calls together his friends and neighbors, saying to them, 'Rejoice with me, for I have found my sheep that was lost.'

Luke 15.9 When she has found it, she calls together her friends and neighbors, saying, 'Rejoice with me, for I have found the coin that I had lost.'

Luke 15.32 But we had to celebrate and rejoice, because this brother of yours was dead and has come to life; he was lost and has been found.

For further reading: Luke 15.1–20 (again!)

Yes I know I've done these parables already but they are so important that they warrant further reflection and the pulling out of an additional strand. I've already noted that these parables speak of a deep care that naturally gives rise to great celebration but they are also, obviously, parables about losing and finding. One of the intriguing features about Luke's Gospel is the way in which he creates deeper insights into Jesus and who he was by the way in which he puts things next to each other. The placing of these three parables side by side evoke, in me at least, a deep reflection on what it means to be lost, and then, what it means to be found.

We begin with different models of being lost. The sheep, the coin and the son are not all lost in the same way. In the first parable, the lost sheep, the sheep wanders off and gets lost by itself. In the second parable, the lost coin, the coin just is lost. It did not, could not, wander off (though it may have felt that way– I certainly think my keys wander off without me). In the third parable, the prodigal son, the son deliberately loses himself. Unlike with the sheep and the coin, the son makes a deliberate choice to go off. The question that arises is when did the losing actually take place? When he went off in the first place? When he lost his money? When he began working with the pigs? What is very clever about Luke's placing of these three parables next to each other is that they become an extended reflection on getting lost. In the light of the sheep and the coin, we are left to reflect upon the extended process of the son's losing.

This is very important. The way in which these parables are normally interpreted suggests a somewhat flat, monochrome view of 'being lost'. People not in the kingdom are lost. There is no doubt in my mind that this is part of what is meant here. The language of sinners repenting and the rejoicing that takes place in heaven when they do repent, all point to these parables being, in part, about sinners' entry into the kingdom. But it strikes me that this is not all. The lost sheep was a part of the herd before it got lost, the coin was one of ten before it was misplaced, the son was a member of the family before he went off. Of course, on one level, Jesus is talking here of members of the Jewish community who became 'lost' by being sinners, tax collectors and prostitutes, but I can't help wondering whether we miss something in these parables by making them solely about those sinners 'out there'.

The multi-faceted view of becoming lost presented by these three parables raises the question of whether they also have something to say to those of us already in the sheepfold, the coin collection and the family. They point us towards the fact that losing can happen in so many different ways, we can wander off, become misplaced or deliberately choose to go off and slowly through a process of poor decisions lose ourselves. It is so easy to become lost both in terms of God and the kingdom but also in terms of ourselves.

Losing is not the whole picture however. The finding is equally important. Again the parable of the prodigal son provides rich material for reflection about how finding takes place. When was the son found? Just as there is an extended process of the son losing himself, so also there is an extended process of him being found again. It begins in the pig sty when 'he came to himself'. This small phrase exacerbates the extent to which he was lost – he was lost even to himself – but then, through a process of repentance, forgiveness and acceptance, he was found again and restored. All of this challenges us to reflect deeply about the small processes that lead us to lose ourselves and the equal, yet opposite steps that are needed to ensure that we are found again, by ourselves, by the communities that love us and most of all by God.

It seems to me that these parables of losing, finding and celebrating challenge us all to become communities that care so deeply about those who are lost that we will go to insane lengths to find them. We need to become communities which are profoundly in tune with the process that leads us to become lost in the first place and also with the process that helps us to return again, found, restored and loved. Most of all we need to become communities that celebrate finding in all its forms, and like Jesus to feast with the people of the kingdom wherever and whenever they are found.

The kingdom of our everyday God is best compared to ordinary things, like seeds and weeds, yeast and bread making, sheep, coins and families. The kingdom is characterized by overwhelming generosity and is always present when genuine celebration, which flows out of love, takes place. The nature of God's kingdom can be best discerned and understood when we compare it to the things of our everyday lives but we must never lose hold of the fact that the kingdom is as much not like these things as it is like them. The kingdom might be like weeds but it brings life rather than destruction to those things growing around it. It might be like yeast but you can't kill it by turning up the temperature. It might be like finding unexpected treasure but you can't steal it.

The kingdom is like all of these things and it is not like them. It is much, much more than them. Most of all the kingdom cannot be tied down, defined, labelled and boxed. It is not for nothing that New Testament scholars struggle to define exactly what the kingdom of God is. The kingdom of God can be likened to a seed but most definitely cannot be held in the hand.

PART THREE

Living Extraordinary Ordinary Lives

5

THE CALL TO
EXTRAORDINARINESS

So far in this book we have been exploring ordinariness: we have looked at unsung, ordinary biblical heroes, at a God who shuns splendour and lives in our midst and at a kingdom that is best likened to ordinary things like seeds and yeast. It is now time to turn our attention to extraordinariness. This does not in any way overturn all the ordinariness that we have explored up to this point. We remain an ordinary people, called by a God who loves us so much that he came to earth to live alongside us in the every day. But it is that calling which summons us into extraordinariness. We don't need to become someone else, or suddenly develop super powers. We don't (necessarily) need to train for years, or become experts in something we are not good at. All we need to do is to respond and to see where God draws us.

We are looping round to return again to pick up a theme from the first chapter, where we looked at the importance of turning aside in the midst of our everyday lives to hear God's call. Now we are returning to ask the question about the extraordinariness to which God calls us in the midst of our everyday lives and to explore what this extraordinariness means about how we live out our lives.

❧

1 Surely you aren't going to send them?

Mark 6.7–13 He called the twelve and began to send them out two by two, and gave them authority over the unclean spirits. He ordered them to take nothing for their journey except a staff; no bread, no bag, no money in their belts; but to wear sandals and not to put on two tunics. He said to them, 'Wherever you enter a house, stay there until you leave the place. If any place will not welcome you and they refuse to hear you, as you leave, shake off the dust that is on your feet as a testimony against them.' So they went out and proclaimed that all should repent. They cast out many demons, and anointed with oil many who were sick and cured them.

For further reading: Mark 4.1 – 8.38

Alphonso X, King of Castile and Len in the thirteenth century, is reputed to have said: 'If the Lord Almighty had consulted me before embarking upon Creation, I should have recommended something simpler.' One of the things I love about this is that, if I'm honest, I often have a similar feeling. If God had consulted me then I would have recommended all sorts of things ... many of which would probably be a very bad idea. It is a good thing that God does not consult us; a whole universe of back-seat drivers could only lead to disaster. This is one of those passages, however, where Jesus really does go against any of the advice that we might want to offer.

In this passage of Mark, he sends out the disciples on their first mission. They are given authority over unclean spirits and are sent out to proclaim repentance and, although it doesn't say so explicitly here, it is safe to assume that they also proclaimed the coming of God's kingdom. So far so good, they are the disciples after all. The mission is surely in safe hands … or maybe not.

One of the remarkable features of this account is not that the disciples are sent out to proclaim God's kingdom but that they are sent to do it at this point of the Gospel. The disturbing and slightly shocking nature of this only really makes sense if you take a step back and read a sweep of the Gospel that runs from chapter 4 to chapter 8. This part of Mark's Gospel is where we begin to encounter something important about the disciples: that they simply do not understand who Jesus is or what he has been sent to do. Mark 4—8 has three boat scenes: one in 4.35–41, one in 6.47–53 and one in 8.14–21. In each of these scenes the disciples demonstrate quite how much they do not understand Jesus. Mark 4.35–41 is the account of the stilling of the storm when, at the end, Jesus asks them: 'Have you no faith?' Mark 6.47–53 is the walking on the water which ends with the comment that they didn't understand about the loaves and the fishes. Mark 8.14–21 reaches the climax of this whole question with Jesus asking the disciples: 'Do you still not perceive or understand? Are your hearts hardened? Do you have eyes, and fail to see? Do you have ears, and fail to hear? And do you not remember?' (Mark 8.17–18). The implicit answer to all of these questions being no, they don't.

Mark 4—8 seems to be a section, then, in which Mark reflects upon how much the disciples do not appear to understand yet who Jesus is or what he has come to do. Would you send them out to proclaim the kingdom? I know I wouldn't but Jesus not only would but did. Where was their training course? How did he know they weren't going to make a mess of it? Did they proclaim the kingdom right? If Jesus had consulted me I would have advised a bit more preparation before he sent them out. Of course, we don't know how much preparation Jesus gave the disciples before he sent them out, nor indeed is it any of my business to know. It seems to me that one of the emphases of this section is that Jesus didn't stop to ensure that the disciples had perfect theology or a wonderful presentation style before he sent them. He simply sent them and they went.

This is not to say that I think we should scrap all theology courses and all ministerial training of any kind. I am passionate about learning of all kinds but I do just wonder whether we have the emphasis a bit wrong these days. It is easy to assume that what we do today is learn and then minister. This is not the model I see here. The word disciple means literally, not a follower as many assume, but a learner. The disciples were called to a life-time of learning and while they were learning, before they had even understood some of the vital things they needed to grasp (like who Jesus was and what he had come to do). Jesus sent them out in service of the kingdom.

This seems to suggest two very important things: you don't have to wait to be ready before you go, and once you have gone there is still more learning to do. Learning and proclaiming, following and serving are all integrally linked. Jesus calls us just as we are and sends us onwards to a lifetime of service for the kingdom, proclaiming, learning, healing and loving, just as the earliest disciples did. Don't wait until you are ready ... go now, there is plenty of time to live into the rest.

2 Forgive us, just like we forgive them

Matthew 18.21–22 Then Peter came and said to him, 'Lord, if another member of the church sins against me,

*how often should I forgive? As many as seven times?'
Jesus said to him, 'Not seven times, but, I tell you, seventy-seven times.'*

Luke 6.37 *'Do not judge, and you will not be judged;
do not condemn, and you will not be condemned. Forgive, and you will be forgiven.'*

Luke 11.3–4 *'Give us each day our daily bread. And
forgive us our sins, for we ourselves forgive everyone
indebted to us. And do not bring us to the time of trial.'*

What is the hardest thing that Jesus asks of us? The list
is probably quite extensive and different for each one of
us but one of the things that must have a place on such a
list is surely forgiveness. None of us finds it easy but children, I think, are particularly aware of how hard it is. As I
watch my daughters screw up the courage to say sorry to
each other, I can never decide whether it is harder to say
sorry or 'that's OK' (our modern equivalent of I forgive
you) ... and that is before we get anywhere near the even
harder task of not just saying it but meaning it.

Forgiveness is, in my view, one of the most radical elements of Jesus' message and I think we often forget quite
how radical it was. Until the time of Jesus, forgiveness
belonged to God and only to God. If you read through
the pages of the Old Testament all the references to forgiveness are associated with God and God's willingness
to forgive us. Forgiveness was also focused around temple worship and the offering of sacrifices in the temple.
There is no reference to the need for one person to forgive
another. Indeed, Israel's law was radical in its day simply because it required God's people to limit their vengeance: 'If any harm follows, then you shall give life for
life, eye for eye, tooth for tooth, hand for hand, foot for

foot, burn for burn, wound for wound, stripe for stripe' (Exodus 21.23–25). Vengeance, the law stated, should only be wreaked in proportion to the sin that had been committed.

The first radical part of Jesus' message was that forgiveness could now take place outside of the temple, and that Jesus himself could forgive sins. This is why in Matthew 9.2 when Jesus tells the man who is paralysed that his sins are forgiven, the scribes claim that he is blaspheming. In their system he was blaspheming. He was claiming to be able to do something outside of the temple that only God had ever done before and that inside the temple. As we all know, however, Jesus didn't stop there. He didn't stop with saying that he could forgive sins but went on to say that we should too.

The Greek word used here is the word for leave behind or let go and the idea it communicates is that we should stop holding on to grievances and hurts and let them go, leave them behind and move on. Hard as it is to forgive others, there is a vitally important reason why we should – our own freedom. The problem with holding on to past grievances is that it locks us into the past, by doing so we build a prison for ourselves that prevents our escape. There is a story about someone called Debbie Morris who was kidnapped in the USA and her boyfriend shot. When she spoke about the experience much later, she said that 'justice didn't heal me, forgiveness did'. That simple little phrase resonates deeply with me from my own experiences. It is only when we can let go of our hurts, that we can find healing, hope and a new future. Jesus told us to forgive one another not because he liked setting us impossible tasks but because he loved us and wanted us to be free.

There is another reason as well, and one that we pray regularly in the Lord's Prayer. The prayer Jesus taught us instructs us to ask that God will forgive us in the same way that we forgive others. Not, as we easily assume, that we should forgive others as God forgives us but the other way around. As with our prayer for the coming of God's kingdom, I often wonder whether we are really listening to what we are praying, and hope that perhaps God might be listening no more carefully than we are. It seems to me to be a terrifying prospect to ask God to forgive us in the same way we forgive others. I always hold out the hope that God's forgiveness of my sins far exceeds my ability to forgive others ... but this is not what we pray for here.

Forgiveness, then, lies right at the heart of our life as Christians and lands in the middle of our ordinary lives. The greatest need we have to offer and receive forgiveness arises in our everyday lives: in the things that we mean to do that we don't quite manage, and in those things we intend not to do and do anyway, and in the things that others said they would do and didn't and said they wouldn't do and did anyway. Jesus' command of forgiveness gets no easier the more familiar it is but it is no less important for all that.

ᔕᔕ

3 Being the Body of Christ

1 Corinthians 12.12–14 For just as the body is one and has many members, and all the members of the body, though many, are one body, so it is with Christ. For in the one Spirit we were all baptized into one body – Jews or Greeks, slaves or free – and we were all made to drink of one Spirit. Indeed, the body does not consist of one member but of many.

1 Corinthians 12.27 Now you are the body of Christ and individually members of it.

For further reading: 1 Corinthians 12.1–31

I have always had a very visual mind. When people describe things, I see them in my mind's eye. Sometimes this is useful, often it is not. I don't have a choice whether I visualize what is being described or not; like it or not there it is! As a result, I have always found myself intrigued by Paul's metaphor of the Body of Christ. Did he, I wonder, have a visual mind or a verbal one? When he talked about all those in Christ being Christ's body did he visualize, as I do, a vast, ungainly, lumbering body or was it more of an idea? I can't help thinking that he might have veered towards the visual, not least because in 1 Corinthians 12 we find ourselves in the middle of a slightly farcical conversation between an eye and a hand and a head and some feet (1 Corinthians 12.21), about who has need of whom.

Not only is the image bizarre, it is also immensely challenging, though probably not quite as much for us as it would have been for Paul's original audience. Paul lived, and wrote 1 Corinthians, at a time when there were plenty of people alive who had seen the body of Jesus. He even makes reference to the more than five hundred men and women, most of whom were still alive, who had seen Jesus' resurrected body. Jesus' body, then, meant even more to Paul's audience than to us. They would have been able to tell you how tall Jesus' body was, what colour his hair was, whether his eyes crinkled when he smiled, and many, many other details. For Paul now to say that those who are in Christ are Christ's body on earth would have been mind-blowing to his audience. Since he was saying that the Christ who walked around in Palestine only decades earlier now has a new body, a body made up of those who followed him and were baptized into Christ.

You could argue that Paul's use of language about being a body (I am desperately trying to avoid the phrase 'body language' which means something else entirely to us!) would have been at least a little familiar to his audience, and this would be true. Members of the Corinthian Christian community who were accustomed to the workings of city states would have been familiar with them being described as a body which needed to work well together. Equally, readers of the book of Ezekiel would have been aware of the great vision of Ezekiel which likens the people of God to a set of dry bones which became a body into which was breathed the spirit of God. What Paul does here, though, is to take this well-worn metaphor a significant step forward, because he did not say that the Christian community was any old body, but a very particular person's body and one that many of his audience would have seen with their own eyes. Paul's language reminds us that our extraordinary calling as Christians is to live out our ordinary, everyday lives as Christ on earth.

The crucial word in that sentence, however, is 'our'. It is all too easy to slip into thinking that I am called to be Christ on earth, and if I fail that all will be lost. Paul's point here is not that any one person is called to be Christ's body but that together, all those who are in Christ, can be the body of Christ. That is why we simply cannot afford for any part of the body to consider themselves unnecessary to the whole. We need all the help that we can get to live out this extraordinary vocation. Christ's own self was so remarkable that it takes every single person bringing the very best of their spirit-given gifts for us to have any hope at all of fulfilling this calling. Just as in Ezekiel, it is God's breath or spirit (in Hebrew and Greek the word can mean either) that brings the body to life and so it is the use of the spirit-given gifts that ensures the life of the body.

Here the ordinary and extraordinary collide. Some of the gifts Paul talks about are what we would call extraordinary, like the working of miracles, speaking in tongues and prophecy. Some are what we might call ordinary, like helping or administration.[11] The point Paul hammers home throughout the whole passage is that all the gifts are vital to the proper working of the body. Having a spirit-given gift and not using it in the body will sap the body of its life. Declaring that someone with their spirit-given gift is no longer needed equally takes the breath from Christ's body.

This wonderful, ungainly, lumbering body of Christ needs every single one of us bringing all the gifts we have to live out this most extraordinary of callings. No gift is too small, none too unimportant or ordinary, each one breathes life into the Body of Christ.

❦

4 Carrying each other's weaknesses

Romans 15.1–3 We who are strong ought to put up with the failings of the weak, and not to please ourselves. Each of us must please our neighbor for the good purpose of building up the neighbor. For Christ did not please himself; but, as it is written, 'The insults of those who insult you have fallen on me.'

For further reading: Romans 14.19–15.7

---

11 Actually the Greek word used here is hard to translate. The NRSV translates it leadership whereas the ESV and the NIV as administration. The word refers to the skill used by a pilot in guiding a ship using a rudder, so neither leadership nor administration quite capture the image.

Sometimes I find myself deeply entertained by the translational decisions made in our English translations. This passage is one of those occasions. I'm sure that the translators did not intend this but, in my mind, the implication of the NRSV translation of Romans 15.1 is that the strong will stand around, rolling their eyes, tutting occasionally and as they do so 'put up' with the failings of those weaker than them. Putting up with something suggests to me somewhat bad grace, barely concealed irritation but a determination to make the best of things because there is no other choice.

I think something really rather different is what Paul has in mind here. He has in the previous chapters been talking about dietary requirements and what you should do when you perceive that others are weak in the faith. In Romans 14.3 Paul says: 'Those who eat must not despise those who abstain, and those who abstain must not pass judgment on those who eat; for God has welcomed them.' What Paul does quite cleverly here is to contrast the strong (literally the able) with the weak (literally the unable). The question is: which is which? The one who eats meat or the one who doesn't? The one who abstains on certain days or the one who doesn't? Paul never tells us. Those who are strong are strong in their own sight. It is quite possible that everyone to whom Paul is speaking here would put themselves in the 'strong' category and their opponents in the 'weak' category. Effectively Paul is speaking to all of us. Anyone who has ever prided themselves on their insights, anyone who has even for a moment felt sorry for or despised their opponents, is immediately in the category of the strong, since we consider ourselves 'able' where we view others 'unable'.

This is where Paul's advice becomes transformatory, since his major point is not that we should 'put up' with the failings of the weak but that we should take up, bear or carry the things that make the weak (the unable), weak. The Greek verb is used elsewhere. Matthew uses it as the verb to describe Christ bearing our diseases: 'He took our infirmities and *bore* our diseases' Matthew 8.17; and Luke uses it to describe taking up your cross and following Jesus: 'Whoever does not *carry* the cross and follow me cannot be my disciple' Luke 14.27. This is no bland putting up with but a much more costly taking upon ourselves, bearing, as Jesus did our sins and infirmities.

What we take upon ourselves are the things that make the weak weak (a word that can equally be translated as the things that make someone feeble, ill, or full of misgivings). What Paul is saying here is that those things which we see as making a person weak are precisely the things that we should take upon ourselves. This is one step further than the old adage that if you don't understand someone you should walk a mile in their shoes (to which the entertaining response is that then you will be a mile away from them ... and you'll have their shoes). This is down to the nitty gritty of living out our lives as Christ's body. Christ bore our diseases to the cross, so we too are to bear the weaknesses of those whom we despise and, as we bear them, we are changed. We become different people, transformed by the action of carrying the weaknesses of our neighbours.

What this all means will be different for different people in different circumstances. With conflict about food, Paul means that those who eat meat should not eat meat for the sake of their neighbours. This won't work with every conflict that we have but it does mean that we should strive to carry the things that we think make others weak so deep within us that they become a part of us and change the way we view the world. This is a truly lived-out expression of being Christ's body in the world.

It is an extraordinary vocation which can only be lived out in the ordinariness of our lives.

ᴄ᷌ᴕᴋᴕᴖ

5 And being weak ourselves

2 Corinthians 4.7–10 But we have this treasure in clay jars, so that it may be made clear that this extraordinary power belongs to God and does not come from us. We are afflicted in every way, but not crushed; perplexed, but not driven to despair; persecuted, but not forsaken; struck down, but not destroyed; always carrying in the body the death of Jesus, so that the life of Jesus may also be made visible in our bodies.

For further reading: 2 Corinthians 4.1–12

One of the major messages of the New Testament is, possibly, also the hardest to stomach. This is the summons to weakness and fragility. It runs so thoroughly against the grain of our culture (and indeed probably against human nature itself) that it is almost impossible to get our heads around, let alone to live out. We live in a world shaped both by success and the call to even greater success. We learn from an early age the sting of the label 'loser' and feel obliged to strive with all that we have to avoid it. People in the public gaze who make mistakes, so often do everything in their power to avoid the shame of having to admit that they might have done something wrong. Everything in our culture pulls us away from failure, or more particularly admitting failure.

Nevertheless, both the gospel and Paul's epistle summon us to a different way of being, one marked not by personal success but by vulnerability and weakness. Throughout the Gospels Jesus calls us to be 'servants' of each other, something which requires us to place ourselves willingly in a position of vulnerability. Paul also adopts the language of being a servant and even a slave of Christ, and even more radically, goes out of his way to remind us of his failings. For example in 2 Corinthians 11.23–33 he gives a positive catalogue of failure including imprisonment, floggings, near death, stoning, shipwreck, sleeplessness, and even having to run away from Damascus by way of a basket lowered over the wall. It is the most bizarre CV you are ever likely to see but tells you something important about how Paul views himself and his relationship with Christ. Paul believes that the more he reveals his own weakness, the easier it is to see Christ's strength.

The passage from 2 Corinthians 4 is another place in which he explores a similar theme, with the vivid imagery of clay jars. Clay jars were the disposable packaging of the first-century world, so it would be odd to put treasure in them, but that is part of the point he is making here. The jars are so ordinary that by contrast the treasure is seen, all the more, for what it is. It is even possible that Paul had in mind Corinthian night lamps that were made of deliberately thin, poor quality clay to allow the light to shine through them (including through their cracks!). If this is the image he has in mind the contrast is between these lamps (made of poor quality, thin clay) and Corinthian black work which was heavily glazed, beautiful pottery. The latter looks gorgeous but all you can see is the pot.

I have always loved the hymn 'Immortal, Invisible, God only Wise', with its ringing line 'Oh help me to see, 'tis only the splendour of light hideth thee', not least because I find it a challenge. Is it in fact true that it is only the splendour of light that hides God? I can't help wondering whether, in reality, it is the splendour of Christians that hides God, and whether we are all more like Corinthian Black work pots than night lamps. Paul's language in this passage reminds us that it is in being truthful about our day-to-day fragilities, about the things that afflict and perplex us, that enables people to see God's treasure for what it is. The point is not that people think well of us but that they can see God.

It is important to remind ourselves, though, that this isn't a manifesto for self-indulgently letting it all hang out. We must all know people who, under the guise of vulnerability, simply use the opportunity to talk about themselves ... all the time. The revealing of vulnerability is not meant to be some call to masochism nor to self-indulgent pessimism, but simply to move ourselves out of the way so that Christ in all his glory can be all the more visible. A simple rule of thumb which will enable us to work out whether the balance is right or not is the question 'Does my life reveal or hide Christ's glory?'

Of course this question takes a huge amount of personal courage to answer accurately. It is so, so easy to argue to ourselves as much as to others that the narrative of my own success reveals Christ and conversely that my tale of woe will reveal Christ. What Paul challenges us to do here, however, is to reflect long and hard about how we live and what we tell others about how we live, with the goal of ensuring that both what we do and what we say about what we do reveals Christ to all those we meet. Paul challenges us to live our ordinary lives with courageous integrity, an integrity that constantly seeks not our own glory but Christ's. This is extraordinary ordinary living of a most unusual kind.

⋯✲⋯

6 A noble lifestyle?

1 Peter 2.12 Conduct yourselves honorably among the Gentiles, so that, though they malign you as evildoers, they may see your honorable deeds and glorify God when he comes to judge.

For further reading: 1 Peter 2.1–12

What comes to mind when you hear the word 'lifestyle'? Lifestyle is a common word these days and can be found widely in, among other things, newspapers and magazines, on television and as a section in bookshops. So important is it that many national papers have a lifestyle section which explores a huge range of things from recipes to clothes, gardens to cars, houses to holidays. It is striking that the more you hear the popular media talking about lifestyle the less it appears to be discussed among Christians. The question of what a 'Christian lifestyle' might be is surely vital in a context so otherwise concerned about lifestyle choices and decisions. In the past a Christian lifestyle was often defined by what you didn't do: in some circles Christians didn't drink, didn't go to the cinema, didn't go to parties or listen to pop music, the list goes on. An increasing number of Christians now recognize that this is the wrong way to go about things. The problem is that as a result we have stopped talking about lifestyle at all.

Although you can't immediately see it from the NRSV translation this passage raises exactly this question. The phrase translated here as 'conduct yourselves honourably' is probably best literally translated as 'having a good way of life' or 'a good lifestyle'. What the author of 1 Peter is arguing is that we are called to think deeply about our way of life and to live in such a way that warrants the description 'kalos'. This is one of those words that is hard to do justice to in English. It can be translated 'good', but the problem there is that good in English carries the hint of moral virtue which does not capture the entirety of the word 'kalos'. Other possible meanings include beautiful, healthy, fine, magnificent and noble.

1 Peter, then, is talking about living a life that is shaped by actions and decisions that are fine, beautiful, noble and good. This seems to me to be all about positive choices not negative ones. It seems to pull us towards a way of life that has woven within it an expectation of well-being for ourselves and for others, of excellence and of vision, of encouragement and inspiration. It draws us towards choices that bring wholeness into our lives. Most of all it calls us to ensure that our ordinary lives are lived out to extraordinary standards that might be best described by the word 'noble'.

It is worth reminding ourselves at this point about the other half of this verse. 1 Peter does not say that living a noble lifestyle will mean that everyone will suddenly recognize our virtue, be won round by our actions and start being nice to us. Instead it says that they will continue to speak evil against us. Nothing will noticeably change but that 'when God comes to judge' (i.e. at the end of all times) they will give glory to God. Giving glory to God happens when we recognize that God is God, and praise him for who he is. The suggestion here then is that our noble deeds will allow our detractors to recognize God for who he is when they encounter him at the end of all times. In other words, people will be able to recognize God from what they have seen of our lifestyle.

Of course the question that naturally arises from this is, what is this noble lifestyle? How can I be sure that I am living it to the best of my capacity? The answer, it may not surprise you to know, is that you have to work that out for yourself. There are no easy prescriptions to be found that help us to say I need to do a bit of this, a lot of that and less of the other to ensure the success of my noble lifestyle. It is your way of life and there is no short-cut to working out what it might mean for you. A useful general guide, however, is to ask the question of whether people will be able to catch glimpses of God from who you are and what you do. Will they be any closer to a recognition of God from their encounter of your way of life? This is a scarily challenging vision of who we might be and what we might do, and summons us to the highest, most positive standards of living.

❧

This chapter brings us back to the paradox that I was ex-ploring a little in the introduction, which is that God both loves us exactly as we are and summons us to a deeper and richer expression of ourselves. God both calls us as we are and sends us to do things which we would say are far beyond us. God both loves ordinariness and at the same time summons us to extraordinariness.

In this chapter we have explored only some aspects of the extraordinariness to which God summons us – one theme which connects them all, however, is that they find their origin and their expression in our daily lives. They are to be found in the living out of our Christian calling, day by day, week by week. What this calling looks like in practice will be different for each person and requires a lifetime of prayerful discernment to come close to work-ing it out, but some of the markers of this kind of liv-ing include being prepared to be sent by God before we think we are ready; being people who dedicate ourselves to giving and accepting forgiveness; joining in with the vocation of being Christ's body on earth and offering our gifts whatever they are for its welfare; bearing the weaknesses of those we consider weaker than ourselves and being transformed by them; and seeking a way of life or lifestyle which reveals God's essence in the world. There are many, many more markers of the extraordinary, ordinary lives to which God calls us, but these are quite a good place to start.

6

GLIMPSING GLORY

It would feel wrong to leave our explorations of ordinary living without looking at what glimpses of glory in our everyday life might be like. What was it that Moses encountered when he turned aside? What gave Rizpah the strength to sit out her lonely vigil on the mountain side? What is the beam of sunlight, the brightness, which is the eternity that awaits you? What is it that transforms us in the very midst of our ordinary living into people able to live out God's extraordinary calling? How do we know when we have had a glimpse of glory? The short answer to all of these questions is that when you have seen it, really seen it, you will know, and you will know without a shadow of a doubt.

Of course, so often we don't really see. We catch a glimmer, the tiniest hint, and by the time we have turned our heads, or managed to slow down enough to register what we have seen, it is gone, leaving in its wake the merest suggestion that there might have lain the treasure in the field. We have already explored, in Chapter 1, the need to be people who can and do turn aside, now is the time to consider what we might encounter if we do.

❦

1 Shall we start the building work?

Mark 9.2–5 Six days later, Jesus took with him Peter and James and John, and led them up a high mountain apart, by themselves. And he was transfigured before them, and his clothes became dazzling white, such as no one on earth could bleach them. And there appeared to them Elijah with Moses, who were talking with Jesus. Then Peter said to Jesus, 'Rabbi, it is good for us to be here; let us make three dwellings, one for you, one for Moses, and one for Elijah.'

For further reading: Mark 9.1–8

Probably the best example of a glimpse of glory, or in this case quite a sustained vision of glory, is the story of the transfiguration of Jesus. Here we get a sense not only of what this kind of encounter might entail but also how human beings often react to it.

One of the questions that always arises in my mind when I read this passage is the question of what Jesus' transfigured body looked like. The Greek word, translated transfigured, is the word from which we get our English word metamorphosis. As a result it implies that some change of form has taken place. The question is, what kind of change was it? Unfortunately, there is no direct answer to this since the Gospels writers simply don't tell us. What they do tell us, however, was what happened to his clothes, information which is not quite as useless as it might first appear. Jesus' clothes, we are told, become a brilliant white. At first glance this feels like entirely unhelpful information. I don't want to know what he had on, you might feel like saying, I want to know what he really looked like. Actually, a description of his clothes might have been the closest the disciples could get to describing what they saw.

The biblical writers regularly struggled to put into words the visions of God that they had. So, for example, in Ezekiel's great vision of God's throne chariot, the prophet described in detail the wheels of the chariot, the arrangement of the creatures' wings and even the dome or firmament on which God's throne rests but when he described the one sitting on the throne, he became suddenly vague. Ezekiel describes the one on the throne as having 'the appearance of the likeness of the glory of the Lord'. You don't get much more tentative than that.

Jesus' brilliant white clothes, however, suggest that what Peter, James and John saw was Jesus in all his glory; Jesus in his full divinity; or in other words, Jesus as he really was and is. Brilliant white garments, throughout the Bible, are associated with God. This is why angels wear white, because they come directly from God and the whiteness of their clothing reminds us of this. Jesus' white clothes here, then, are a reminder of his divinity. The transfiguration may have been a vision of Jesus as he would be, risen, ascended and glorified. It might have been a vision of him as he will be when he comes again in glory, but what it certainly is, is a vision of who Jesus really was. Glimpses of glory are those moments when, even for a moment, the veil is pulled aside and we gain a vision, however small, of who God really is and how he views the world.

Peter's response to this vision was gloriously human. My natural reaction whenever I get a glimpse of God is to say 'Why can't it be like this all the time?', and then to strive to return to that fleeting moment for more of the same. Peter, somewhat prosaically, proposes building works. Admittedly in Mark's Gospel they were only tents (the Greek word used means temporary shelter or tabernacle) but nevertheless Peter moved to make the experience as permanent as he could. Having seen the true nature of who Jesus was, he had no desire to move on.

This is to miss the point of such an experience. It is entirely natural once we have caught a glimpse of God to stay there yearning for its return but the point of all of these experiences is that they are, to a greater or lesser extent, glimpses. They need no structures permanent or otherwise built around them, because after them we are sent onwards, down the mountain and back to our everyday lives. Or if we use R. S. Thomas's image of the sun illuminating a field, the very last thing we are meant to do is to hang around that field waiting for the sun to come back out again, or to build an elaborate structure that will allow the sun's rays to be particularly magnified the next time they appear. Instead we are to be ready to recognize the glimpse for what it is when we see it, to drink it in with all that we have, to savour it and then to go on living our normal lives; lives that now will be both the same as ever and transformed utterly by what we have seen and experienced.

⤜✳⤛

2 Infectious glory

Exodus 34.29–33 Moses came down from Mount Sinai. As he came down from the mountain with the two tablets of the covenant in his hand, Moses did not know that the skin of his face shone because he had been talking with God. When Aaron and all the Israelites saw Moses, the skin of his face was shining, and they were afraid to come near him. But Moses called to them; and Aaron and all the leaders of the congregation

returned to him, and Moses spoke with them. After-
ward all the Israelites came near, and he gave them in
commandment all that the LORD *had spoken with him*
on Mount Sinai. When Moses had finished speaking
with them, he put a veil on his face;

*For further reading: **Exodus 34.1–35***

Probably the most sustained encounter with glory is that
of Moses receiving of the law in Exodus 34, where Moses
receives the details of the law on the top of the mountain
before descending to reveal it to God's people waiting
below. Exodus stresses the frequency of Moses' encounters with God (passages like 'whenever Moses went in
before the LORD to speak with him, he would take the veil
off, until he came out' Exodus 34.34, imply that Moses'
ascent and descent were a regular occurrence). One of the
striking features of this account is the infectiousness of
God's glory.

Something happened to Moses during his conversation
with God. The Hebrew is a little unclear and apparently
seems connected to the word for horns, and was translated as such by the Latin vulgate. This caused some early
translations to translate this as Moses' face was horned
(see for example the Douay Rheims translation: 'and he
knew not that his face was horned from the conversation
of the Lord'), which in its turn gave rise to some depic-
tions of Moses with a fine set of horns on his head. It is
now widely accepted that this is the wrong translation
of the passage; disappointing though it might seem to
be forced to remove antlers from our mental picture of
Moses, it is highly unlikely that this is what the Hebrew
means here. Much more likely is that when the Hebrew
says that 'the skin of his face sent out' it does not mean
sent out horns but sent out rays like the sun.

This is a significant tradition since it points to the fact that encounters with God, such as Moses had, are transformative. It suggests that glimpsing glory is not just important in its own right but because it changes who we are. What seems to have happened to Moses was that the time he spent in the company of God caused his face to shine; Paul in 2 Corinthians 3.7–18 assumes that this means that he has been infected by the glory of God. It is not an enormous leap. Tradition has long associated glory with shining light (and later post-biblical tradition developed this into the depiction of halos around holy people), so the shining of Moses' face is highly likely to be the shining of the glory of God. This may seem to be a fanciful idea until you think of people you know who have spent many hours placing themselves in the presence of God. Although their faces do not actually shine out light, luminescence is a good description for the difference of their faces. I have had the privilege of knowing a few such people, and for want of a better description, I would say that their faces do shine. This reminds us of something very important in this tradition, which is that time spent in God's presence, catching glimpses of glory, are not just important in their own right but because they change who we are.

Glory is one of those words which is incredibly difficult to define but it communicates something rich and deep about who God is. Just as the transfiguration revealed Jesus to be who he really was, so the glory of God communicates something deep about who he is. The word *kabod*, when used of a person describes a reputation that brings them honour – and hence often describes their wealth. So for example, Genesis 31.1 talks of Jacob's wealth which he took from Laban as *kabod* ('he has gained all this wealth (*kabod*) from what belonged to our father'), and in Genesis 45.13 Joseph tells his brothers literally 'to tell my father all my glory' (translated as 'You must tell my father how greatly I am honoured in Egypt', in the NRSV). God's glory then is his reputation in the world that brings him honour, or in other words encounters that reveal who he really is.

The difference between God's glory and our own reputation is that human reputations often make others jealous; whereas God's glory transforms people to be more like him. Unlike human glory, God's glory is infectious, it transforms us to be more like him so that when God then sends us out – as he always does – to do his will in the world, we leave his presence changed, different people from when we arrived, and as a result all the more able to do what he sends us to do.

࿓

3 The lifting of the veil

2 Corinthians 3.15–18 Indeed, to this very day whenever Moses is read, a veil lies over their minds; but when one turns to the Lord, the veil is removed. Now the Lord is the Spirit, and where the Spirit of the Lord is, there is freedom. And all of us, with unveiled faces, seeing the glory of the Lord as though reflected in a mirror, are being transformed into the same image from one degree of glory to another; for this comes from the Lord, the Spirit.

For further reading: 2 Corinthians 3.7–18

The companion passage to Exodus 34.29–33 is 2 Corinthians 3.7–18. This remarkable passage by Paul is an extended reflection on Exodus 34. In fact, so intriguing a reflection on Exodus is it that some scholars have argued that it is an example of a synagogue sermon by Paul which he has re-used here in his argument to the Corinthians. The whole passage plays with the idea of the veil that Moses placed over his face. This raises the question of what the veil was for. In my mind it also begs the question of what it looked like – was it made of heavy material or light? Coloured or plain? Could he see through it or not? Sadly, there are no answers to this so we will have to content ourselves with reflecting on what it was for instead.

A natural, and quite widespread, assumption is that the veil was to prevent the people of Israel from being frightened by God's glory shining from Moses' face. Both Exodus and Paul remind us of the terror that the people experienced when they saw the glory of Moses' face Exodus 34.30 says that 'When Aaron and all the Israelites saw Moses, the skin of his face was shining, and they were afraid to come near him', and Paul glosses this in 2 Corinthians 3.7 as 'so that the people of Israel could not gaze at Moses' face because of the glory of his face'. The problem is that, although there is no doubt that the people are terrified of the glory, that doesn't seem to be how Moses uses the veil – nor in fact is it how Paul understands it. In Exodus, Moses came down the mountain unveiled and told the people what he had heard while his face was shining to its fullest extent, he then put the veil on his face (see Exodus 31.35). Paul understood this as Moses covering his face so that the people could not observe the glory fading (2 Corinthians 3.13). The idea is that the longer Moses was away from God's presence the more the glory faded until there was hardly any left. The veil, it seems, was to prevent people from seeing and remembering the fading glory, rather than the most powerful glory.

Paul uses this as the springboard into his own theology

of glory, a theology which is remarkable and inspirational. He likens turning to Christ to Moses' experience on the top of Mount Sinai. This is his first and radical departure from the tradition. Exodus 34 stands in the long and important Old Testament tradition which recognizes that only a few important men (like Moses, Elijah and Isaiah) could encounter the living God, and that when they did so they were far away from normal existence. Moses was on the top of Mount Sinai, Elijah on the top of Mount Horeb and Isaiah in the temple. Here Paul likens the experience of everyone who turns to Christ, man or woman, priest or lay, important or not, to that of these few, significant men. *Anyone* who turns to Christ, finds their veil taken away and becomes like Moses standing in the full glory of God.

So we all, he says in 3.18, have unveiled faces because in Christ we are permanently standing in God's glory. The need for a veil to hide the fading glory is no longer necessary because the glory never fades. In fact, in Christ the glory goes in the opposite direction. It no longer fades but increases from glory into glory, and as it does we, like Jesus at the transfiguration, experience metamorphosis (the Greek word is the same as what happened to Jesus) as the glory constantly deepens, broadens and enlarges.

For me the absolute pinnacle of this remarkable verse is Paul's description of how we behold the glory of the Lord. The word used (*katoptrizomenoi*) can mean either to gaze in a mirror or to reflect as in a mirror. This suggests that, we who are in Christ, no longer need to trek to the highest mountain in order to encounter God's glory since we encounter it every day, in our ordinary lives. As we live out our lives in Christ, we reflect God's glory; as we reflect God's glory we see it reflected. As we see it reflected, we reflect it some more, and the glory grows from glory into glory as this happens.

This passage then takes us on an astonishing journey from where we started. We started with Moses with the burning bush turning aside to encounter God's in-breaking into his world. We end with the recognition that this same quality of experience is a natural part of our ordinary life in Christ. Turning to the Lord leads us to stand permanently unveiled in the presence of the infectious glory of God, a glory that gets ever richer the more we behold and reflect it. This truly is a vision of extraordinary, ordinary living in which we no longer have to rely on special men to trek up a mountain to encounter God's glory but can encounter that glory every day of our lives.

❦

Paul, as he so often does, moves us on beyond our wildest imaginings. We are accustomed to thinking about God's breaking into our lives with dramatic experiences like the burning bush, or simple quiet experiences like the sound of sheer silence; we expect to look for God's glory in the full revelation of Christ at the transfiguration or at the giving of the commandments on Mount Sinai. In 2 Corinthians 3, he pulls us up short and reminds us that glimpses of glory – or more accurately ever expanding reflections of glory – are to be found in and through those who are in Christ. To our list of possible places where we might encounter God, we must add our brothers and sisters in Christ – and indeed ourselves.

What we see, however, remains the same whether we see it on the top of a mountain or in the face of our brothers and sisters in Christ, and that is glory, a glory that reveals something profound about who God is. It is this glory that infects us, transforms us and sends us onward to live out our extraordinary, ordinary lives in Christ.

EPILOGUE

Ordinariness lies right at the heart of our Christian faith. The God, whom we worship, is truly an everyday God who time and time again breaks out of the gilded palaces we create for him and meets us instead in our everyday lives. This God cares more about people than about grandeur. He is more concerned with justice than fine worship. This God is more likely to be found with mud and dust, than with gold and jewels. This God yearns to give us everything we need to thrive. This God reveals his glory both with dramatic fire, thunder and lightning, and in the sound of sheer silence. This God breaks into our lives and transforms us from glory into glory.

We are most likely to encounter this God in ordinariness, in our everyday lives and in the people that we meet day by day. So often we miss glimpses of God's glory not because they are not there but simply because we fail to notice them. We know that God is not to be found in this kind of situation or with that kind of person, and so we fail to look, and go on our way unchanged.

Reflecting on ordinariness throughout the Bible reminds us that we need to learn to be self-confidently 'ordinary' people who can celebrate God in the ordinary things of life, who can look for and encounter God in the everyday, who expect God to meet us while we wash up, get on the train or talk to our friends. We need to be alert to the possibility that this event or that encounter might just provide us with a glimpse of glory. We need to become people who, like R. S. Thomas can recognize that moment which is for us the pearl of great price or treasure in the field, and to turn aside, and in doing so to encounter the eternity that awaits us.

BIBLICAL INDEX